ENDORSEMENTS

It is in the heart of every Christian leader to wish that their children would follow in their steps and one day take up their own cross and follow Jesus into Christian ministry. Seeing this become a reality is very wondrous and gratifying, but seeing this happen and continue under a strong anointing of the Holy Spirit is all the more wonderful. I am very proud of my daughter Lori, who is pastoring in Birmingham, England and championing the tenets of our biblical evangelical faith, and doing it from the foundation of the Father's great love. And yes, she continues to experience revival fire and the Holy Spirit's wonderful, life-giving Presence.

Thank you, Lori, for such an honoring account of the recollections of your early years and your surprise and delight with the revival that later came and was ours to lead and enjoy. I know you are as proud of me as I am proud of you.

May this book encourage you, the reader, to be inspired and committed to see revival pass on to the next generation, and then the next. And may the PKs and the MKs of this world be encouraged to "…contend earnestly for the faith which was once for all delivered to the saints" (Jude 1:3 NKJV).

John Arnott
Catch the Fire Ministries, Toronto

I think the most exciting thing that any parent can experience is watching their children become successful in living their lives fulfilling their destinies. As parents, I think we sometimes fear that our dysfunctional behavior will so influence the child that they may not become all that Father has envisioned when He created them. When I read Joshua's chapter in *Sons of God's Generals* about living his life with legends, I experienced again the pride of a parent who has had the privilege of seeing their child overcome the obstacles of life and embrace their identity and live their destiny. For Joshua, we always knew he was to become a warrior, but life for him was often characterized by the term *rebel*. Success in life is not always guaranteed just because you grew up in a home with good parents. You still have to make your own choices in response to their parenting model.

Reading this book, I feel, will help the reader to understand that life with legends does not necessarily mean you will have a problem-free life. In his chapter, Joshua helps you understand the whole heart of a prodigal son trying to live life outside of the comforts of a good home. Other children of generals in this book express what life in their environment was like with their legends of legacy. You will laugh and cry and be given the opportunity to judge each general, but I pray that you will have grace for each of us and that you will embrace the courage that this book offers to help you live and become a legend in your own right. Thank you, sons, for writing this book, for the honor you have shown to us generals. You make me proud to be placed into a position to watch the next legends develop into generals.

Trisha Frost
Author of *UNBOUND* and cofounder of Shiloh Place Ministry

Mary is an extraordinary person, truly a woman of destiny, with an equally extraordinary calling on her life. It has been a joy and honor to be her parents, to see her mature over the years, and to witness how well she has handled the pressures and expectations of having parents who are pastors and also founders of Harvest International Ministry. (HIM is an apostolic network of churches that is comprised of over 20,000 churches in over 50 nations.) As hard as it has been for her to see her father travel so often, Mary has also traveled the world and these travels have gifted her with a unique perspective and passion for the poor with a heart to eradicate injustice and systemic poverty globally. We love Mary deeply, and as with all of our adult children, we are very proud of her.

Che and Sue Ahn
Sr. Pastors, HRock Church
President and founder, Harvest International Ministry

Lineage and legacy are important relational commodities in the Kingdom of God. A culture of honor is an admirable goal but only if it includes honesty, dialogue, and mutual exchange. I could not be more pleased with the edgy, transparent musings and observations presented by my oldest son, Justin Goll, for this strategic book. I laughed, I cried, I applauded. He wrote with an equal dose of candor and respect. His chapter alone is worth the price of this book! May the true joining of the generations come forth!

James W. Goll
Encounters Network—Prayer Storm—GET eSchool
Author of *The Seer, The Lifestyle of a Prophet,
The Lost Art of Intercession* and many others

Sons of God's Generals is an engaging look into the lives of the sons, in my case the firstborn, of some of today's generals of the faith. How did the absence of their fathers and in some cases the mothers from the home for significant periods of time affect the children? How did the fame of the fathers affect their children? How did the ministries of the fathers and mothers affect their sons and daughters? How did the passion of the fathers and mothers for the Kingdom of God affect the children? Told from the perspective of the now adult children in a way no one else could tell it. Read and learn what it was like living in the family of generals of the faith.

Randy Clark
Founder and president of Global Awakening and
the Apostolic Network of Global Awakening

It is a sheer delight to recommend this book. God shines through Crystalyn's descriptive writing and we laughed and cried as we read her powerful chapter.

Through the years, the Lord has been directing us and showing us what He is most of all interested in. We pray, as you read this book, that God too will cause you to reach out more and more to the ones closest to you, and to the nearest desire of His heart—family.

Heidi and Rolland Baker
Founders, Iris Global
Authors of *Always Enough* and *Expecting Miracles*

You and I will read together for the first time Yana's story: our family story, as seen through her eyes. Are we anxious, excited, nervous, proud? Of course we are! We wonder how our seemingly normal life that was turned upside down by the Holy Spirit really affected her.

Global travels, road school, seeing the nations, visiting the poor, loving the gypsies, feeding the multitudes in Africa with the Bakers… all has obviously given her a rare perspective. With the Lord's help, it has molded her into the beautiful young woman, wife, and mother that she is today.

We couldn't be more proud of her as she is enjoying being a mother, a 'foodie', a writer, an artist, and yes, our one and only daughter. We look forward to many more of her creative expressions. After all, aren't we all involved in telling the greatest story of all time?

Love, Georgian & Winnie Banov
Founders, Global Celebration

SONS

of God's Generals

SONS
of God's Generals

Unlocking the Power of Godly Inheritance

JOSHUA FROST

DESTINY IMAGE® PUBLISHERS, INC.

P.O. Box 310, Shippensburg, PA 17257-0310

"Promoting Inspired Lives."

This book and all other Destiny Image, Revival Press, MercyPlace, Fresh Bread, Destiny Image Fiction, and Treasure House books are available at Christian bookstores and distributors worldwide.

For a U.S. bookstore nearest you, call 1-800-722-6774.

For more information on foreign distributors, call 717-532-3040.

Reach us on the Internet: www.destinyimage.com.

ISBN 13 TP: 978-0-7684-0427-2

ISBN 13 Ebook: 978-0-7684-0428-9

For Worldwide Distribution, Printed in the U.S.A.

1 2 3 4 5 6 7 8 / 18 17 16 15 14

DEDICATION

We, the children of the generals being written about in this book, wish to honor these generals by dedicating this book to them. Thank you, Moms and Dads, for loving us unconditionally, for seeing our purpose and being the example that motivated us into our own path of becoming generals for the next generation.

CONTENTS

FOREWORD

This is a thought-provoking yet fun book to read. *Sons of God's Generals* is an honest look at growing up in the home of various spiritual leaders. I found myself laughing out loud, as well as having tears come to my eyes in reading this manuscript, all because of the transparency and insights of these very real people. What you're about to read is honest, heart-warming, and sobering all at once. Much wisdom is to be gained from the *Sons of God's Generals* for anyone wanting to truly leave a legacy to the generations. Thanks to Joshua Frost for the vision for this book.

Bill Johnson
Bethel Church, Redding, CA
Author of *When Heaven Invades Earth* and *Hosting the Presence*

INTRODUCTION

The question that I am often asked when people realize that I am the son of Jack and Trisha Frost is, "What was it like growing up in this household, and how did it affect my relationship with God?" People are interested in other people of notoriety and how they became such people. Their individual life story seems to motivate others in their own life journey, especially if that attainment has been beneficial to help others in their life situations. So after being asked this question throughout my life, I started pondering the idea of this book. I found myself wondering what it was like for others who had grown up under the care of generals in God's army. What were their struggles as they were trying to find their own identity in life? How did growing up in the home of a general influence their own outcome? This book answers these particular questions and so many more. It will take you on a journey through the lives of the sons and daughters of modern-day Christian generals in God's army.

A different son or daughter of a modern-day general has written a chapter in this book answering each of these questions and sharing their journey of finding God through their individual relationships. My desire for this book is for you, the reader, to learn from our experiences of growing up in these households so that you can take what we have learned and use it in the transformation of the lives of your family. Good and/or bad experiences, the stories are entertaining to say the least and useful to say the most. I hope that this book will encourage you, cause you to smile, and help you to relax as you go about the will of your Father as you, too, experience life with your family.

Many blessings,
Joshua Frost

CHAPTER 1

SON OF A GENERAL

Eric Johnson

John Adams once said, "I must study politics and war, that my sons may have the liberty to study mathematics and philosophy, natural history and naval architecture, in order to give their children a right to study painting, poetry, music, architecture, tapestry, and porcelain."

As an adult reflecting on my upbringing and now having my own children, I have numerous thoughts that come to mind about what it was like for me, my brother, and my sister to be raised by our dad and mom. Often people ask me what it was like being raised by Bill and Beni. My usual reply is, "It was pretty normal."

Usually when someone asks that question, they are contrasting it to their own experience or what they have heard. I think it's important to note the normalcy of it all because I think we can tend to idolize or picture some surreal scenario that we want to experience. I want to take the time to emphasize the normal because it really was and is. My parents are incredible people; they are not just my parents, they are my heroes and really good friends. They are very down-to-earth and very passionate about the things of God.

I think often we look at generals in the body of Christ, and we don't grasp the reality that we all have similar common denominators. We eat, sleep, play, work, breathe, and share life with others. I think sometimes we can create this idea that it's impossible to be like someone we admire or respect. The truth is, once you've seen it or heard it modeled, then you can have it, too.

The Realization

I am surrounded by a very strong Christian heritage. On my dad's side of the family, I am a sixth-generation pastor, and on my mom's side, I am a fourth-generation Christian. A joke I often tell people is I had five options growing up, and it was either to be an apostle, prophet, pastor, teacher, or evangelist. My home was filled with crazy love, freedom, and respect. There was no tension or arguing. I have no recollection of my parents ever fighting or arguing. They just didn't do it. For me, this is my normal; I know nothing else.

It wasn't until halfway through high school that I realized that not all of my friends were raised in healthy homes. For some reason, it didn't occur to me that my own upbringing wasn't typical. For most of my life up until that point, I thought that what we had was normal for everyone. An interesting moment for me was when it became apparent that it was not, and I began to realize that the many things I took lightly were the exception. Around this time I understood that I was in a unique situation and I needed to embrace my own upbringing and heritage more seriously.

We have been very blessed to have a family lineage that is saturated in Christian heritage. Not a day goes by that I am not thankful. I do fully understand this is not the case for many. For me, it is a place that I get to stand with my life, decisions, and gifts so that I can give it to my children and their children. (If you want more insight on this topic of spiritual inheritance, please see my book, *Momentum: What God Starts Never Ends*.)

Be Authentic

Another revelation that hit me at some point in my teens was the so-called stigma of being a "pastor's kid." That was never something that I lived with or faced in any way in my life. I would hear stories of other pastors' kids who would get extremely rebellious toward their parents, who were in church ministry, and would resent the church and the role of the pastor.

My parents were the same people off stage as they were on the stage; they were the same in front of people and the same when they weren't in front of people. We didn't experience a different mom or dad when they were at home. I personally never questioned what was more important, the church or their kids. It was undoubtedly us. At the time I was not aware of all the things they did to demonstrate this. Sometimes it was the simplest things like driving us to school every day or eating breakfast and dinner together. When we were really young, Dad would read us two stories from a book that talked about animals and the spiritual truth about them. My mom would cut my hair or make me clothes. So when they were taking care of the people as pastors, we got to see them love people the way they loved us. We got the best of them, and that enabled them practically and spiritually to be incredible leaders and pastors. The life they lived was demonstrated to the church, and it was authentic.

The importance of being authentic is often not emphasized enough. Authenticity creates trust. You know what you are going to get when you come into contact with an authentic person. There is no guessing or wondering who they are and how they are doing. Our home was filled with genuine authenticity, which created a high level of trust and respect for each other.

When you create a value system for authenticity on a personal level, then you get excited when people around you are authentic as well. Freedom and respect are results of an environment that allows you to be you.

Free to Be Ourselves

One of the fruits of a home that was built on freedom and respect was there was no need to control or dictate the course of life. Whenever you walk in the freedom of who you are, you have little need to control others and would rather serve what is on the hearts of those around you. I often share with people that I can't recall many conversations in which I was told what to do with my life, whether it was about my career, who I would marry, where I would live, etc. There is one instance when Dad and I went to a meeting where Mario Murillo was preaching, and during the meeting my dad simply mentioned to me, "Make sure you watch Mario, because you may be in his shoes someday."

We had lots of intentional conversations that showed me it was important that I pursue my passions, whether they were smuggling Bibles in China at age 13 or pursuing baseball. It was really clear that it was important to them that I stayed in tune with my heart and what was going on in my life and went after it with a passion. I had an incredible amount of freedom when it came to my actions as long as my attitude was healthy. Perhaps the reason I'm a huge advocate for being empowered and trusted to make great decisions in life results from this freedom and trust.

I have a very strong conviction that God trusts you more than you trust yourself. One of the happiest moments as a parent is when I see my kids making great decisions without our input. It is a great sign that we are raising them well. It was very obvious to me when we kids would make great decisions because Dad and Mom would celebrate it and cheer us on. Our home carried a deep level of trust for each other, and freedom was the place we lived from.

Passion Is Contagious

It was always important in our home to do what you love to do and to do it with a passion. We had no long conversations to make sure I understood this. Rather, it was lived out. Whether the normal daily things in life or a journey into the heart of God, it was done with a lot of passion and pursuit. One of the things that is common knowledge about my parents is their passion for worship. On Sunday morning when it was time to worship, it was normal to see my parents with their eyes closed and hands raised in passionate worship to God. More than just singing a few songs, worship was the focal point of their life, and it meant abandoning themselves to the King.

A stirring moment for me was when I was around junior high age, and my dad was recording an album in a studio a few hours away from our home. We made a family trip up to this studio for a few days. One moment, all of us were in the control room along with the studio engineer, and on the other side of the wall was my dad sitting at a piano. He was playing, singing, and weeping all at the same time. Listening to him had a deep impact on me. I realized that this thing called *worship* was more than just an action; it was the way we do life. I was forever marked.

Mountain Chapel was our church for two decades, the place we all grew up and learned about community and the Kingdom. In our little mountain town, we were known as the crazy church, and others referred to us as a cult. That one always made us smile. For us, worship was a way of life, the highest priority to God. The culture of worship for us was created there, week after week, day after day. Being a part of a culture of worship continues to shape us more than we realized. My brother and my sister have major roles of leading people all over the world in worship. That was birthed in Weaverville at a little church called Mountain Chapel.

We often talk about what helps to grow leaders in the body of Christ, and there are many things that help to accomplish that. We don't realize how much worship plays into it. I don't worship so I can become a great leader. However, it's clear that giving my life to worshiping the King has helped me to grow and be able to lead the body of Christ. It is here where my heart is shaped and formed to the one that is the source of all life. This is the one place where I can come as I am, whether I bring a sacrifice or a dance to the King. Worship shapes how we see God, which, in turn, shapes how we live life.

Passion is contagious. It is transferrable by seeing it and living life with each other. When you see someone who carries passion for something, be it worship or fly-fishing in the Trinity Alps wilderness, it gives you permission and freedom to pursue things that are in your heart. My wife often reminds me that when I get into a hobby, I *really* get into it! This kind of passion was instilled in all three of us kids so much that it ended up playing an integral part in how we pursued God on our own and how we live out our lives.

Discipline with Love

"I'm disciplining you because I love you," were words that I heard quite a few times in my childhood—usually before any of us kids was going to be spanked or grounded for some length of time. In that moment, those words never made sense to us. My young mind was not able to fully understand the depth of those words. However, as the disciplining got less and less and farther and farther apart, it became really clear what those words meant.

We weren't disciplined for behavior as much as we were for our attitude. Our actions were the result of our heart. When our heart and attitude got out of hand, then our behavior demonstrated that. Any time I would do something out of anger, rebellion, frustration, or any other similar emotion, it was essentially because I didn't watch or guard my heart. There was always a little sermon before we got disciplined. This little sermon would usually go with the words, "I'm disciplining you because I love you." How true are those words today. This simple action instilled in us a deep desire to guard our hearts, which helps us be who we are today. Now in raising our own children we find ourselves repeating those words: "I'm disciplining you because I love you."

Love for Diversity

From 1995 to 1997, I attended a Bible college for two years. Every morning all the students were required to go to chapel for a service, which was always an interesting experience for me. Every day in chapel we would have a different speaker. So it became normal that one day a speaker would say something like, "If you aren't going to the nations and leading people to the Lord, then you aren't doing anything." Then the very next day a different person would say, "If you are going to the nations and leading people to the Lord, but you aren't even reaching your own neighborhood, then how can you live with yourself?" It was quite challenging and very comical.

The funny part for me was when we went to class right after chapel. All of my classes were Bible or ministry focused. My fellow classmates were in some form heading toward church ministry. Whenever we would have a speaker in chapel, the professor would usually take a few minutes to allow us to discuss our thoughts about the message that was given in chapel. The following discussions would make it really clear that there wasn't much value for diversity. The most opinionated students would always speak first and make their point really strong. I began to realize that "being able to eat the meat and throw out the bones" was challenging for a lot of my classmates. If the message didn't fit a certain way of thinking, they would reject the speaker and the message entirely.

This was another area that my parents set a strong example—to always find gold in people, no matter what. I've heard my parents say, "If we have a hard time with 95 percent of what someone said, then we will only focus on the 5 percent." They had a tremendous value for diversity in people. I believe this is one of the keys to favor with people all over the planet that they have—they genuinely love people and the diversity in them. When you walk in the freedom of who you are, it's really hard to be threatened by diversity. Rather, you find joy in seeing the diversity, and you are always able to find meat to eat.

Leading by Example

I want to end with this thought—lead by example. Brian, Leah, and I are very blessed to have a set of parents who led by example. All of the things that are mentioned in this chapter, plus many stories and situations not mentioned, were things that our parents lived out. Their need to control our outcome was minimal, but in a unique way, they did shape the outcome of who we are because they lived and demonstrated a life that is authentic, inspiring, and tangible.

Everything you just read in this chapter was intended to share with you our lives that we are living. It is how we have been shaped into what we are today. My desire is that when you read this, you will find keys and truth that will help you in the way you live life because once you have seen it modeled, then you can have it as well. I bless you from our house to your house, and may the Lord bless you and keep you.

CHAPTER 2

WHAT IT WAS LIKE

Crystalyn Human

People often ask me a question that in my mind has become infamous: "What was it *like?*" They are undoubtedly referring to my upbringing. What was it *like* to grow up in Africa, and not only that, but with parents who have great demands on their time and have become celebrities in the charismatic Christian world. People ask this question with sincerity and genuine interest, so I feel a small stab of guilt when my shoulders start hunching and I start mildly stuttering some kind of poor answer that includes things like, "There were good things... there were difficult things...I wouldn't have traded the experience...." These kinds of responses offer little substance to those who ask, but I've always felt it was simply too broad of a question for me to handle properly. How do I sum up my childhood in a succinct and meaningful answer? What is it that people are most interested in? I used to joke that I should write a book entitled *What It Was* to hand out in response to people's questions, instead of my awkward and vague, stammering replies. I never imagined I actually might do it. Interestingly enough, the opportunity presented itself to write this chapter, so here I'll do my best to describe a bit of my experience and include a few of the highlights and struggles I encountered while navigating my own identity and journey with the Lord.

My focus will be our time spent as a family in Mozambique, a country in southeast Africa labeled the poorest nation in the world at the time we moved there. It had been ravaged by years of war, first one for independence from Portugal and then a brutal civil war. Mozambique has since been labeled the most peaceful country in Africa with one of the fastest-growing economies. That fact alone should encourage you that literally anything is possible. I was, however, already eight when we moved there, so here is a brief overview of our prior life in Asia, England, and our brief stay in the US.

I was born in Hong Kong, the fourth generation on my dad's side to be born in Asia. The city name is all that's listed on my passport because it was a British colony at the time, and therefore neither England nor China. My mom was swollen all over with toxemia during the pregnancy and was told I would be born damaged or dead, but miraculously I was born completely healthy. I've been told about the nine flights of stairs we took up to a cramped apartment in a somewhat sketchy building in one of the most crowded square miles on the planet. But my only vivid memories of those first several years in Hong Kong involve loving Chinese food in pre-school, practicing writing Chinese characters, and walking through packed and colorful streets watching giant puppets dance around.

Then for three years in England I attended a private British school, developed a British accent, and experienced my first real ministry memories. My parents started a church there and ran an outreach where

I remember being bundled up at night, warmed by tinfoil-wrapped baked potatoes I would help pass out to weathered homeless men on the street. London is also home to my first memory of being extremely tired at the end of a night church service and either grabbing on to my parents and informing them it was time to go or falling asleep on the floor. Again, our family of four lived in a small apartment that was constantly filled with all types of people, including polished lawyers who worked with us and would become our first African missionaries, and also the poor who needed warmth and community.

Although my parents have since told me how poor we actually were during the earlier days of their ministry, I never noticed lack of any kind. I have very fond memories of England. Like a lot of my life, it was a filled with vastly different types of people and experiences ranging from frolicking with our rough collie in Hyde Park to going to a posh private school to the aforementioned chilly nights of street ministry to home groups where I caught lice more than once. When I think of our eclectic group of family friends who felt like my extended family, I realize early on I was exposed to both rich and poor, the polished and the rough around the edges, and therefore learned by my parents' example to be no respecter of persons. My mother was raised in an upper middle class family in Laguna Beach and has become as comfortable and confident in remote bush villages as in five-star venues or hotels. I like to think some of that versatility has rubbed off on me. She also has an extraordinary ability to make people feel loved and honored regardless of status, and she is incredibly fun—traits I love and feel I've learned so much from.

Notoriety is something no one in my family has ever sought, so it's rather hilarious that my parents' names have become as well known as they are. I have vague memories of my parents discussing moving to Africa, and thinking to myself it sounded like a rather logical thing to do. After a brief year-long stay in a California mountain home, Mom had finished her PhD and we were ready to move again.

My brother Elisha and I flew to South Africa via Malaysia with our dog Nicky in tow, hopped in Mom's truck, and spent the night with a family who served us warthog pie. Like most things at the time, eating warthog seemed different to say the least, but not overly strange. I just tried to not imagine Lion King's Pumbaa. The next day we drove to the South African and Mozambican border, where in later years, while waiting for our car to be searched, my parents were offered cows for my hand in marriage on at least one occasion.

I vividly remember the day I crossed the Mozambican border for the first time. As soon as our wheels hit Mozambican soil, everything changed. Paved roads gave way to dirt ones filled with cratered potholes, and buildings gave way to open fields. We sang "Shine Jesus Shine" to pass the time, and our voices shook uncontrollably with each word while our truck flew over the bumps. Abandoned, rusting, shot-up vehicles littered the side of the road the entire way to the capital city of Maputo. They were remnants from a recent war conflict and reminders of the continued danger. My father not long before had miraculously escaped having his car shot through by bandits on his first trip down that same road. His car broke down at the border but after he managed to turn it around it began running perfectly. Meanwhile the car that drove in ahead of him was found ripped apart by bullet holes. Despite the car skeletons dotting the Mozambican landscape, I never once felt afraid. It simply never crossed my mind that I wouldn't be safe, even when later down the road some experiences tested that theory.

Peace in the Storm

I believe that when you follow a calling from God, even if you make some mistakes there's provision for your kids. My parents tell stories today that sound justifiably intense, but I remember feeling a lot of peace in those moments. Honestly, I think the same sense of safety I felt crossing into the war-torn border of Mozambique sheltered me during the earlier years in some potentially dangerous situations. Our first children's center was in Chihango, a plot of land outside Maputo. My parents were given the responsibility of caring for the street kids there who were essentially starving under so-called government care. In Chihango we often heard gunshots and witch doctor chants outside our house. I remember the chanting more than I do the gunfire. I grew up knowing the demonic was real because I saw it all the time. Watching the demonized get delivered was a fairly common occurrence. The chanting was eerie, especially because it was directed at our destruction, but I knew it wasn't something to be afraid of. Our God was surely more powerful. That's not to say we weren't in a battle. Multiple kids woke up in the night feeling physically strangled and oppressed during that time. Today some of those same street kids cared for in Chihango are now empowered adults helping lead other Iris centers.

Another potentially frightening experience involved a car wreck in the rain after a trip through Kruger National Park. Our truck rolled in the air three times and landed upside down in a ditch. In shock, I started yelling, "I can't feel my legs!" It might have been the scariest thing my mom has ever heard, but once a suitcase was lifted off me I was able to stand up and calm down. My brother was lying down, bleeding from head to toe from shards of shattered glass. He's one of the least dramatic people I know in panicky situations and has a bone-dry sense of humor, so he was still cracking one-liners, calm as ever. Staff from a local mission saw us and stopped. They took us in and miraculously managed to salvage our completely totaled truck. We dubbed it Lazarus, a name that stuck through the following years of rough use. That mission in White River, South Africa, has remained connected to Iris to this day. Two years later I removed a shard of glass from my knee, leaving behind my only scar. My dad was speaking at our Chinese home church in California at the time of the accident, and when he shared what happened people literally came up to the altar and threw their car keys on the offering plate. It was that kind of humbling gesture that always reminded us we had a global family cheering us on.

Certain experiences have made me believe perhaps the Lord honors courage and faith whether or not wisdom is involved. Perhaps surprisingly, the only time I've been personally threatened with a weapon was while riding on a *chapa*, a Mozambican bus that typically crams on as many people as humanly possible. I was taking a ride to the city with a female missionary, a few elderly female visitors, and a couple of our Mozambican youth. A group of ominous-looking men at the front of the bus suddenly rushed to the back where we were sitting and effectively blocked our exit. A few of them simultaneously pulled out knives in front of us while some others pulled out screwdrivers and other tools. I suppose advanced weaponry wasn't readily available. One reached around inside my jacket demanding a phone, one grabbed the elderly woman's necklace next to me, and one demanded the missionary's purse, which contained not an inconsequential amount of money for Iris.

Funnily enough, despite our proximity to the knives, no one gave in easily. The missionary, frightened but stubborn, grabbed her purse and said, "No." I grew annoyed and said repeatedly I had no phone on me. And then came the best moment of the day—the white-haired woman on my left started gnawing on the man's hand that was wrapped around her necklace with her teeth while saying, "In the name of Jesus, no!" Now this is not behavior I would recommend to visitors. When we asked her about it afterward, she proudly announced that if her necklace were to go it would be sold as a donation to missions and not otherwise. I've witnessed on several occasions a sense of injustice rising up in people who are being physically threatened and clearly overpowered. I think sometimes fighting for justice simply looks like love and sometimes it looks like courage to go through a bit of a battle. Clearly you need to listen to the voice of God in the moment, but regardless of whether we showed faith or stupidity, seconds later we slowed down and the gang of men raced to the front and jumped off the moving bus. We gratefully continued on our way.

It was while still in Chihango that I experienced an undeniably African moment. I was walking alone near our house on a red dirt road that snaked through fields of long yellow grass when a small boy who was also alone walked up to me and took my hand without saying a word. He was probably only three, and scabies covered his head. He silently walked with me all the way back to my house. It was the first moment I remember having my heart connect with an African child and feeling like that was it. I was done for. Africa would always be a part of my life. His name was Valentino and his father had brought him to us. His mom had been beaten to death by bandits while Valentino was with her, and his dad didn't know how to care for him on his own. Later his brother Davidinho came to live with us as well, and was miraculously healed after we watched him almost die on a hospital bed from cerebral malaria. I was instantly in love with them. The last time I spoke with Valentino years ago, he had grown into an incredibly kind and intelligent young man who loved the Lord.

Eventually the government had enough of our blatant Christianity and forced us out of our first center, so we packed up and left in the middle of the night. But in my mind it was just a rather spontaneous trip to our house in the city. When you live that lifestyle, going with the flow is just kind of a necessity. In the following weeks many of the kids from our center had nowhere to go, so we filled our courtyard and house with beds. My mom often shares about the first time we saw food multiplied, and it was during this hectic period of time that it happened. It seems to be a proven principle that the more desperate you are and the more your life requires God to show up, the more He does. All I knew was a woman came over to bring us a cooked meal and not only did my family eat, all of our kids ate also. I don't even think the miraculous part of it dawned on me until later.

It was in this desperate season that God again provided a miracle in the form of land for another children's center in Machava. The land had no electricity or running water, one had to be cautious of land mines, and both adults and kids, including me, would constantly get sand worms in their feet. A Brazilian missionary couple named Jesse and Raquel Braga came out to run that center, and their daughter Sarah became one of my best friends in the world. Eighteen years later, after almost being washed away in the 2000 floods, which her family and the Iris kids walked out of chest deep, the Bragas are still there, and Machava is one of Iris's most organized, well-kept, beautiful centers. It is also a worm- and malaria-free zone. We've witnessed so much of God's goodness there and still we are constantly in a fight. Only a few weeks ago a gang of twenty men broke into the Bragas' home, fired shots in the air, and stole everything of value while they miraculously hid. Other missionaries and college visitors were shoved against walls with guns pointed at them. This gang has had a reputation for extreme violence and despite the obvious trauma this caused, the fact no one was shot or seriously hurt is an utter miracle. I can safely say the brave men and women who live their lives on the mission field are in great need of constant prayer and encouragement.

Practical Life

When I say Chihango was outside the city of Maputo, I mean it was an hour away down some of the worst dirt roads I've been on. I'll just say those early rides to school didn't lend themselves to sleeping. At one point on the journey from the city to the center, our trucks had to pass through a stretch of road adjacent to a sandy cliff that barely allowed for the width of the truck. I wondered repeatedly if it would one day drop into the ocean.

Many people ask me about my education growing up, often assuming I was homeschooled, which, once you get to know my parents and their schedule, is slightly comical. I think it's a testament to God's goodness, knowing how much they value education, that not long after we arrived they were contacted by a couple of teachers who had taught at my dad's boarding school in Taiwan, and asked if there was a need for an American missionary school in Maputo. It was a strict school with high workload standards and a focus on college prep. The students I knew who wanted to attend university in the United States performed satisfactorily on their SATs and were well prepared.

Before the Christian Academy of Mozambique was officially founded, however, Elisha and I attended a South African school for a semester. We had an eventful first day before we even made it to the school. It was close by, and the quickest way to get there was to walk through a local market, the type of place where you buy a live, squawking chicken for dinner. My mother, brother, and I left the house and were about to enter the market when a Mozambican woman came running to stop us in our tracks and urge us to turn around. My mom had befriended women in the market while learning Portuguese, and one recognized us. Riots had broken out, and we would have walked straight into them and more than likely been beaten and robbed, because at the time there were very few foreigners in the city and crime rates were high. Thankfully our new friend warned us away. Suffice to say we got to school via another route, and aside from a watch-stealing incident, walks became less eventful.

My first Mozambican friends lived on the street where we rented our first house in Maputo. They would come to our courtyard to play and taught me my first Portuguese words while they attempted some English ones. They brought clams from the nearby ocean, smashed them open in front of me and ate them from the shell, insisting I do the same. When we moved out to Chihango I had my first experience with more rural village kids who would surround me and stroke my blonde hair and touch my skin. It was overwhelming at first, but pretty soon I wasn't as much of a novelty. I befriended some of the girls at our center and learned you can play quite a few games without fully speaking someone's language. One day we were all at my house while my parents were gone and I wanted to pierce my ears like them, so they gathered around with needles and Vaseline and we all started praying that it would go well. But I kept jumping back from the needle. When my mom came home and heard, she made sure I had my ears pierced in a more sterile South African environment within weeks.

One of our first missionaries there was a kind but gruff-looking man missing his front teeth whom we nicknamed Machete Bill. I feel he deserves an honorable mention. He was an incredibly loyal man who met my parents in Asia, and after they took a faith journey into a Malaysian prison in Penang and witnessed to his stepson, he vowed to join them in Africa and serve their vision. He was an ex-military man who scared away some thieves that visited him in the night at our center, first by acting insane and running around the room flailing his limbs, and later by decorating a coconut with a face and stabbing it with a knife. My parents had to ask that he refrain from going on land mine searches in our trucks filled with kids along for the ride. He built himself a cage around his bed to ward off the bats and got his nickname from being frequently sighted in a field during the day sharpening his machete.

I learned cross-cultural communication from a lot of people, but perhaps best from my Brazilian friend Sarah Braga. Brazilian missionary families absolutely played a huge role in my upbringing. If it takes a village to raise a child, then they were my village and I am ever thankful for them. I began staying with Sarah when my parents traveled, so we tried to come up with things to do while stumbling through learning each other's language, things that included creating obstacle courses or finding frogs. She felt like my partner in everything growing up, and when my parents began traveling more, her family absolutely became my second family. I was constantly immersed in Brazilian culture, almost as much as Mozambican culture, because they all tend to congregate together. They do community really well, perhaps more so than any other culture I know, and Brazil sends out missionaries to every Portuguese-speaking country in the world. Sarah and my other Brazilian friends were around for so many good and bad moments growing up, too many to mention here. She's taught me so much about vulnerability, loving the Lord, and being an honest and loyal friend.

When we started another children's center outside the city in Zimpeto, our home for the majority of my years in Mozambique, every

Wednesday night my mom would go do street outreach in Maputo and inevitably bring home kids to live at our center. They would shower at our house and generally my brother or I would give away some of our clothes. Once we had a boy newly brought in from the street in our living room, a boy who owned literally nothing. Mom asked if I had anything I'd like to give away, so I went into my room, and after some deliberation I brought back my big stuffed Pumbaa from Disneyland, the same one I tried not to envision while eating warthog. Elisha and I learned from my parents to give things away easily and know we'd be provided for, so much so that once he was down to his last shirt before he finally made a comment. Zimpeto was home to water gun wars with kids and late-night basketball games, and I'm pretty sure I've attempted to climb every tree on the expansive property.

After working on logistics for months, my dad was able to get our first miracle Cessna plane into the country, a plane that endured years of bush outreach trips. We would take family trips to South Africa for supplies, the land of hot water, cheese, and air-conditioning, during which he taught me to help fly. He let me pull back for takeoff, read some of the instruments, and take over for a while, but I have yet to land a plane. Unfortunately, more than one person has been made sick by my zero-gravity practice maneuvers during which my dad would float pens in the air. It's still a goal of mine to get a pilot's license one day. Looking back, it's a bit surreal that I got to fly a Cessna airplane to my braces appointments.

The Struggle

When people ask me what it was like, I assume some want to know what it was like to have parents constantly pulled on by masses of people who rely on them. Probably our biggest struggle as a family was the need for more alone time. I had loving parents who led busy lives and assumed responsibility for a lot of people. They were in high-intensity situations all the time, having never really been through inner healing, so they had to learn, sometimes clumsily, to navigate all that in their relationship and in our family relationships. I did notice something changed about them, although I can't say exactly what, after they came back from a trip to Toronto. It was clearly a good thing, but suddenly my mom became a sought-after speaker and began traveling more. It was a struggle sometimes, and one we've had to process through together.

I actually didn't fully realize the busyness was too extreme until years later when friends started helping me process it, and my mom started telling me they had made some mistakes with their time and she needed to ask for forgiveness. It was a revelation that, shockingly enough, I actually did need healing to break off some of the insecurities that stemmed from that time.

I don't believe spending too much time apart from family is at all a necessary side effect of missions, or even that in the name of sacrificing for the poor you should think that it's normal. I don't even think it has to be normal to feel stressed by a stressful environment or demanding situations. It's possible and clearly preferable to feel balanced and at rest in God in the midst of a storm. I think I have amazing parents who simply didn't have certain relational skill sets until later in life, including setting up healthy boundaries and slowing down to work through painful moments instead of trying to maintain normalcy through busyness.

Most families I know need healing in certain areas from generational and personal struggles. In our case I think those were magnified and intensified sometimes by the high-expectation environment that we were in all the time. I love my parents, I'm grateful for them, and I'm grateful we have the continued opportunity to grow into healthier, more relationally connected people. It's been an ongoing healing journey for all of us, I think, and a chance to celebrate the redemption of God.

I feel the need to point out we did have typical family dinners and movie nights that often involved my dad powering up a generator, because electricity was so sporadic. For fun, besides South African getaways, we loved Kruger Park, tennis, and beach days to name a few. My mother is among the most loving and generous individuals on the planet. She is generous in every way, both in resources and in the way she constantly gives of herself and shares her heart with the world and with the individual. She's admitted to using busyness in work and ministry as an excuse to run away sometimes, and now encourages us to embrace healing and become the healthiest versions of ourselves.

My father is a wise man who could have taught at universities or maintained a comfortable job, but with my mom has pursued the living gospel around the world. He's actually rather quiet and understated, enjoying long conversations over a table with family or close friends, dialoging an issue for the sake of engaging the mind and considering the other side. Sometimes it's infuriating. Not unlike other men in the family, he can be a perfectionist and isn't always verbally expressive, although he has let me know I'm perfect—an obvious lie. As you can imagine, the Holy Spirit and a near-death experience have had a huge impact on his life and made him a freer person. I have no doubt he'd do anything for us. He's never held money tightly, and when he hears Mom's given away something outrageous, he pretends to act surprised for a second and then joins in for the faith ride of continued provision.

Maybe if I had grown up in the west and grown up again in Mozambique more difficult things would come to mind. But Africa is all I knew and I loved it. I mean, aside from a few too many spiders, scorpions, centipedes, and even snakes. Specifically, it's when these heinous things made it into my room that it became too personal. An eight-inch spider with red legs on your wall is just slightly traumatizing. Although I did drama and sports in school, I didn't have many extracurricular opportunities, so sometimes I've envied people who feel incredibly adept in one area because they grew up doing it their whole lives. That being said, my life experience plays a part in everything I do, and I wouldn't have traded it.

One of the hardest things I've been through is watching my parents get sick, but it was when they were close to death that God moved in the most powerful way I've seen. My mom's been near death multiple times, one time notably when doctors thought she had MS, and again with a serious staph infection that prompted one doctor who lacked appropriate bedside manner to tell her to write her tombstone. Some of you may know she was healed while preaching in Toronto after being almost too weak to make it to the stage.

After going to Congo, Dad had post-traumatic stress syndrome coupled with malaria and mini-strokes that fired in his brain. Like almost any person who has grown up in ministry, I'm not one to over-spiritualize anything, but honestly it felt like a demonic principality was at work. He lost his memory for at least three months, grew lethargic and was pumped full of medication after being told his brain had shrunken and his organs were shutting down. After being prayed for daily by people around the world, being taken off his meds, and being pumped full of nutrients in Germany, he experienced radical transformation in his body, mind, and spirit. He came back a healthy man with restored memory and a vibrant personality, and is now flying our new ten-seat, turboprop plane, a miracle plane that has been his dream to fly. Hearing that I should prepare myself not to have my parents around is without a doubt the scariest thing I've had to hear, and their recoveries are the most radical miracles I've ever witnessed. I know they couldn't do what they do without the prayer that covers them from around the world.

My Spiritual Journey and Identity

Like a lot of Christians I know who had Christian parents, I don't remember a precise moment I got saved. I remember my mom reading children's Bible storybooks to me in London and praying with me, but I couldn't say exactly when it happened. Over the years I've experienced some radical moves of the Holy Spirit, and also some quirky mixes of human "stuff"—be it pain, insecurity, or pride woven in there—but to me that's not the main point. What I find remarkable is even early on before I had experienced renewal myself or had much context for it, I never questioned whether it was God. I had a genuine love for the Lord early on, and I loved to sing and worship from the time I was little. In early high school I was involved in a dance ministry group with a number of Brazilian friends at a local Brazilian church, and we would minister at other churches as well. It was a meaningful experience to grow in the Lord with young peers and be accountable to friends in a really communal setting.

I watched the videos my parents brought back from Toronto with another one of my best friends, also a Brazilian, named Ruama. We were immediately impacted by what we saw. When we talked about it at school, I learned that not everyone shared our opinions that the type of emotional intensity you see in renewal could be from God. Those of us from Iris were quietly known as the strange ones. Later on I lost a couple friendships over it, but I also saw good friends from school who had never experienced the Holy Spirit in a powerful way fully encounter Him.

When I finally went to Toronto I had really high expectations, and I was lying on a floor one night realizing that I felt nothing at all. I wasn't laughing or crying uncontrollably. I wasn't hearing anything. I got up fully depressed and thought, "Wow, maybe God isn't real." A crazy thought, given our family history, but it was how I felt at the moment. The next morning I went to the conference anyway, and hypocritically enough even started praying for people before a young woman next to me named Shara grabbed me and asked to pray for me. What followed was a prophetic unleashing like I had never experienced, during which she called out the fact that I had "questioned the existence of God." That's all it took for me never to do that again. One night of questioning who He was, and He revealed Himself in an undeniable way. Shara has become part of our family and remains a strong prophetic voice in my life.

I've heard that hunger for God is a gift, and I know that to be true. It's something you can't do on your own. You can't get yourself so excited and worked up that you're suddenly passionate about God. The only thing I can say—and something Bill Johnson talked about in Bethel School of Supernatural Ministry—is that in the Kingdom, the more you eat the hungrier you get. The more you experience of Him, the more you'll want Him. I really cherish a few specific times of intense hunger for the Lord, those seasons of real intensity and acceleration in my walk with Him. I want to always remind myself to stay dependent, to ask for a constant awakening of that hunger, and to not grow overly content with what I've already experienced.

One of those intense seasons with the Lord began during my senior year in high school. My cousin Marissa came to live with us and volunteer for the year out of a conservative Calvary Chapel background. We both had radical encounters with the Holy Spirit and began practicing every spiritual gift we'd heard about. We practiced the prophetic and did prophetic art even though I don't draw. I would strum the five chords I know on guitar and we would sing as many worship songs as we could learn. If we heard worship music going on in the Iris center somewhere, we would literally run out of the house to find it. We would find ourselves laid out at any moment in the Presence of God laughing or crying, having visions of heaven in our rooms, at the church, in the visitor's center. I feel like God supernaturally taught us a lot about His Spirit that year. It was immediately after that season when I traveled to Mongolia and Brazil to preach and started seeing real breakthrough when I prayed for people to get healed.

When God breaks your heart for a country or a calling, I believe it's a supernatural thing. It's a gift because you feel such a connection and intimacy with His heart. India is just one example of a place God gave me a passion for a long time ago. I feel like during that year I was able to see just a glimpse of His heart for a nation, just a fraction...and it was life changing. My hope is that every Christian would experience something like that. I'm not a stranger to feeling called to something and then questioning it later when it doesn't make a lot of sense, when you have obstacles in your way, or when you feel you're not hearing the

Lord like you used to. One of my biggest spiritual questions has been asking, "When do you pursue something with everything you have despite opposition, and when do you rest and wait for the Lord to be your defender and open the doors?" Of course, I know in my heart the answer is personal relationship with Him, a relationship I need to nurture and rely on at all cost.

In my life, navigating my calling has been an interesting journey overall. Often I've felt a deep internal pressure to "change the world" before I'm thirty. It's been a self-inflicted pressure, possibly reinforced by some people but not by my parents. I've endured many a "prophetic word" from well-meaning people that sound more like they're guessing what I need to hear based on what they know of my family rather than listening to God. Occasionally that's made the conference crowd feel a little unsafe. Of course, I've also received *much* needed encouragement along the way and allowed myself to be okay about feeling called to more than one area and learning to recognize which season I'm in.

Growing up, all I wanted to be was a missionary. Early on I wanted to become a doctor, but when I started radically experiencing the Holy Spirit, I decided what I cared about was seeing people encounter Jesus and getting healed on all levels. So I went to Bethel School of Supernatural Ministry after high school. The Lord started speaking to me about creative arts and the nations when I was seventeen, and reminded me of that a few years later when I felt a bit at a loss about what direction to take in school. When I consider how often I had a camcorder in my hand as I grew up, ready to host some fake documentary or try to make people laugh, it's not actually so surprising that I ended up feeling called to the arts as well as missions. I studied media and communications in college before landing in drama with a minor in international relations. I have a passion for storytelling and continue to study acting in Los Angeles where oftentimes my husband and I are producing or editing either small film or music projects. Acting has helped me come alive creatively and is both frightening and the most fun imaginable.

When I look back at meeting my husband Brock, an incredible man and anointed musician and songwriter, it's remarkable how the Lord simultaneously instilled in him a love for missions in the Third World and instilled in me a deeper passion for the arts and for artists. We spend the majority of our time at our home in Los Angeles, in Mozambique, and in Knoxville, Tennessee, running with some of our most-treasured friends who also happen to be epically gifted music and media makers. Now we have a vision to highlight and partner with artists in places where their talent and passion have been stifled by any number of things—lack of resources, hunger, or the inability to dream of a future. Linked with Iris and United Pursuit we've started our focus on musicians in Mozambique, but envision working with future filmmakers, actors, and other artists in Africa, India, and around the world. We've realized that wherever we are the vision is the same— to encourage artists and friends toward their dreams and see people encounter the love of God through relationship.

The Inheritance

Many people may not know that Iris was founded as a dance and drama ministry in Asia, born out my parents' dream to use the arts to spread the Kingdom. After an early focus on science, my father became a gifted writer and photographer, so he appreciates our desire to tell visual stories. My mom was a ballet dancer and actress who gave it up in pursuit of her missions calling. It's not hard to see the artistic flair in her. My parents have been really great at giving me encouragement and grace to clumsily, at times, navigate though my own passions and calling. It's a process that never feels over, but I know I've inherited both a passion for the creative and a generational missions mandate from them. It's amazing to me that, after my mom's sacrifice in those early years, God is inspiring this generation to revisit that passion for the arts and run with it. It's something I see happening not only in people I know, but on a huge scale. Ever since Brock and I were married in 2008, we've felt a tug between the Third World and the West and believe there's a massive bridge between the two that doesn't just mean resources from the West go to provide for the poor. It means that those who have been hidden will be empowered, walking in dignity and recognized for who they really are and what they have to offer the rest of the world. It means we get to see an incredible exchange of strength and gifting take place.

I am continually experiencing radical generational favor in my life. I married a man who carries an incredible amount of favor and destiny on his own life, and that has made me a better, more radically blessed woman. I feel like our biggest mandate—one confirmed by one of the most influential words spoken over our lives—is to steward that favor as best we can and to forever remember to know and love Him well, and from that place to love those around us well. If I find myself wondering what stewarding favor looks like, I can rely on the conviction that, at least in part, it looks like always remembering to serve the poor and the broken in some capacity. Biblically it's a no-brainer, right? I need to consistently ask myself if I'm living a life dependent on God and taking risks or if I'm getting too comfortable.

I will be ever grateful for my upbringing, for my astonishing parents, for their motivation and boldness to follow their calling as a family, and for the way growing up in Africa has forever required of me more compassion and open-mindedness. One of the things that impresses me most about my parents is the fearlessness they've always shown in pursuing God's purpose for their lives and how fulfilled they are now doing exactly what they were meant to do. Years down the road, I want to be in my 50s and 60s and beyond, knowing I took the path God asked me to take and I was unafraid. I know their experience has pushed Brock and me years forward in some areas, enabling us to learn things more quickly and less painfully so we could begin our journey in a healthier place. In other ways, I still feel like I have so far to go and so much to learn from them. I'm often curious where this journey will take me next, but I'm learning to let my insecurities go and focus on God's overwhelming goodness in my life, the things He speaks over me, and the boldness that is my inheritance.

CHAPTER 3

THE WAR FOR INHERITANCE

Justin Goll

When I think of my parents, James Goll and the late Michal Ann Goll, I am drawn to a photograph taken in the 1970s. Recently married, Mom and Dad are wearing denim overalls, wading through a stream in rural Missouri, leaning on each other. My dad's left arm is draped over my mom's shoulders; my mom's right arm hangs around my dad's back. They are treading downstream to find the right spot for my dad to baptize her. What an amazing generation has gone before me! I only pray my generation will be found as faithful.

What can I write about my parents that hasn't already been written by their ministry colleagues and friends? Their exploits ran over continents. Their books multiplied across languages. There were great obstacles overcome and tremendous encounters with God's power. And yet there is something very simple at the core of their lives—friendship. Before the electricity and controversy of "The Kansas City Prophets." Before mom's missions to Africa. Before the angelic encounters. Before all of that, they were friends to God and prized Him above all else. And despite being gifted in some divergent ways, they were lifelong friends, *best friends,* to each other.

Of course it wasn't all roses! As the firstborn, I got a front row seat to many a marital spat (what Che Ahn calls "intense fellowship"). These are real people with tempers, insecurities, and who don't like mushrooms! And that brings me to what I am grateful for the most. I didn't get perfect parents. In fact, I can't imagine having learned as much about God if I had. What I did get were *teachable* parents, parents who pursued the Lord with their whole hearts and who let God change them over and over again throughout their lives.

The War for Inheritance

Now it's one thing to grow up with godly parents. It's another thing entirely to step into a family inheritance of faith, to acquire the *spoils* of past victories. There are few things that God enjoys and the devil hates more than multiple generations linked together by the desire for God's presence. An old Catholic teaching even declares that while the mission of the church is to extend the Kingdom of God across geography, the mission of the *family* is to extend His Kingdom across *time*.[1]

Of course, there is no inheritance without relationship. So I've set out to tell a tale about relating to my dad, my mom, and through it all, my God, who gave the gift of my parents to me in the first place. First, Dad.

Part I: My Dad, the Prophet

My dad is the warmest, most generous, and most complex man I know. He is a giver—I can think of no better way to describe him.

He gives what he has, whether that is little or that is lots. With dad, there are always gifts being given, prayers being declared, and advice being offered—whether you want to hear it or not! There is always a relative he is thinking of, a young leader he is encouraging, a conflict between friends he is mediating. And he is a man of contradictions. He is extremely loud; he is sensitive. He loves proper etiquette; he loves to break proper etiquette. He's a goofy Holy Spirit drunk; he loves structure and theology.

He is ever involved in the messy lives of people, always helping someone navigate the relational mire. My dad and I, both being strong-willed persons, often clashed as I grew up, but in adulthood I have grown to appreciate the man and the values that forged him. More than his spiritual gifts, I will always be marked by his love and servanthood of others and his commitment to his family.

Prophetic Parenting

As you might have guessed, my first experience of prophecy was not in church. It was at home. I could never tell you the first day I heard it, but as far back as I can recall, I knew that my dad had seen visions of what would happen to me in my lifetime. Everything from career to gifting—not to mention a few prophecies about the end times—was already clearly laid out for me before I even gave 30 days' notice in the womb. Like Zechariah naming John the Baptist, dad had received my name from the mouth of an angel. And the Lord specifically told him that I would "love the arts and history" but that one day I would choose history over the arts.

Now, may I make a request, dear readers? Some of you have perhaps started to think, "That's too much information for a child to absorb."

Right you are! But please let's bear in mind that when I was growing up there was no rule book called *How Prophets Should Deal with Their Vivid Dreams and Visions Concerning Their Children*. In fact, the prophetic movement was, in many respects, in the same stage of life I was in—infancy. I was a guinea pig in an experiment called "prophetic parenting."

The Family Dream Conference

Every morning my family would wake up and have the Family Dream Conference in the living room. "Did anyone have a dream last night?" Dad would ask.

My sister GraceAnn, about three at this time, would sometimes throw in something fun, like, "I had a dream about the circus!"

And then Mom would speak up. She would start describing a dream, and it would be a long one. My dad would get out the tape recorder, shake his head, and mutter to himself, "Amazing." By the time mom finished, his blue eyes were lit up with excitement.

Then I would say, "I had a dream too!" And what would follow would be maybe a dream from God, maybe a drawing I'd made, maybe an image from my imagination. These things were hard to distinguish as a kiddo, but because having dreams was what was rewarded in my family, I felt I had done something good. After all, I saw those sparkling blue eyes turn my way.

Such was life at that age. At five years old I "invited Jesus into my heart" at our church's fall festival. But even after that, I still knew very little about who this God was other than that He was the giver of dreams and that He gave His dreams to *special people*. This half-true idea about God's character would soon be eclipsed by another idea: God can knock you over.

God Can Knock You Over

Churchgoing had always been a gauntlet. Adults I didn't know would approach me so they could get a word with my prophetic dad, and the air of ulterior motive was unnerving. Then, trying to leave church at a decent hour was a joke. After service, clumps of prayer-seekers would form around both my parents. All very inconvenient for a seven-year-old boy who wants to go to Godfather's Pizza and play the arcades!

When our congregation started delving deeper into themes like persecution, my annoyance with church turned to fear of things I was too young to understand. Unbeknownst to my parents, one church member even told me that we Christians would one day confront a tyrant whose minions would shoot us in the head if we did not renounce Christ. At the ripe age of seven, I was ready to stop going to church!

A truce developed with Mom and Dad involving my tolerating church as long as I could draw on sketch paper and speak to no one. The truce kept the peace until one Sunday an incident sent my relationship with not only church, but God, into a tailspin.

Since my dad's primary aspiration at the time was fostering the prophetic movement, I had become accustomed to seeing eccentric men proclaim things about the end times from the stage. The preacher for that particular Sunday was a guest speaker who looked like he would be no different. However, that would not prove to be true. After some initial remarks, this man walked down the platform steps, reached ground level, and suddenly launched his hand toward a man sitting in the nearby aisle. The seated man shook violently, as if struck by a seizure, and fell to the ground. The energy of the room hit a frenzied pitch. Several people began groaning loudly in their seats. The guest speaker touched three more people who all collapsed like the first man.

Most young children's understanding of Holy Spirit "manifestations" is limited, to say the least. I thought the man had unmitigated power to knock me over, to even take away the function of my limbs if he wanted. I was seated with my parents about fifty feet from this spectacle, and the terrifying truth hit—he was coming toward me. The prophetic men who talked about the end times were no longer confined to the stage. Like a lion let loose from his cage, this man began walking closer and closer as men and women fell down in droves around him. He came within twenty feet, and suddenly I cried out inside, "God, leave me alone!" Immediately, a cold sensation came over me. The man stopped his approach. When that silent, angry prayer filled my soul, something changed that I could not describe. I no longer knew if God was on my side or was like that man who was out to get me.

A Spirit of Fear

From that day on for many years, I believe I was deceived by a spirit of fear. Our pastor would occasionally call for the congregation to extend their hands to pray for a matter. In my mind's eye, I would see white light emanating from the hands of these seated people, but I would see gray light—neutral—coming out of mine. My dream life followed the same path. After my experience with "the man of power," I dreamed rarely, if at all.

In middle school this deception bloomed into a decisive cynicism about anything spiritual. My parents had become international leaders in the prophetic scene. Both had traveled the world extensively, praying for thousands of people, fasting, and teaching Christians about intercession. Occasionally they would have a group of intercessor friends over for a prayer meeting. Let me tell you, these people were binding and loosing and binding again just for good measure. I, of course, thought this was ludicrous! After some meetings focused on combating demonic influence in our neighborhood, I sarcastically remarked to my mom, "What are you casting out of the land today?"

Glimpses of Love

Despite my conviction that God was none too kind, there were several moments growing up where God reached out, got around the protective shield I had raised against Him, and gently touched me. The first time I recall experiencing the *pleasure* of God's presence, I was nine. I was attending the mandatory chapel at my school when the worship leader started playing "Holy and Anointed One." Because it was what "good kids" did, I sang along:

Jesus. Jesus. Holy and anointed one.
Your name is like honey on my lips.
Your spirit like water to my soul.

Suddenly a warmth filled my chest. This sensation remained for several minutes. If there's one thing I recall about not *really* knowing God, it's the anxiety. My mind was often captivated by fearful thoughts. But for that pinch of eternity I felt peace.

That little dab would have to do me for a while. The life of a family in Christian service was full of uncertainty, ministry partners coming and going, and then, of course, the fallouts. One such fallout, the details of which I'll spare you, led to my family packing up and moving to another state. My parents loved me deeply, but in the midst of this chaos my very real spiritual battles flew under the radar.

Independence

As I became a teen, it became painfully clear to my parents and to me that my interests were not lining up with the prophetic word God had given before I was born. Now, *overall* the word had eerie accuracy—I did passionately love both history and the arts—but I was decidedly not choosing history as my desired career, as Dad said that I would. Furthermore, coming from a central Missourian family with Holiness Movement roots, I rather doubt my parents imagined that "the arts" God had mentioned could mean *movies!*

I talked about becoming a professional film critic or a scriptwriter. My dad's surprise, and sometimes discomfort, was palpable—things were not going according to plan! Conflicts erupted over my interests. But the real story wasn't about my vocation but about my desperate need to feel like I had more power over my own future than a prophecy of my dad's.

This struggle with Dad magnified the tension in my soul about God. Who was God? Did God, like the man of power I encountered at age seven, have a desire to control me? And if I was *fated* to eventually choose history over the arts, then why even bother with a career in filmmaking?

Forgiveness

By the time I hit sixteen, something happened that I can only attribute to the sovereign hand of God. I began to *crave* forgiveness, and I began yearning to extend forgiveness to my parents. If only I could. But that would require change. And after all the "moves of the Spirit" and the moves of the home address, I did not like change.

In the year 2000, I finally found the key I had been searching for. That fall my whole family flew to Washington, D.C. for "The Call," a massive twelve-hour prayer event. A total of 400,000 believers assembled to intercede for the nation that day, but I, of course, hung back at the hotel as long as I could. Finally, I decided to make an appearance. When I arrived at the grounds where these thousands were praying, I saw something that would change my life forever.

One of the leaders on stage began to speak about how the Lord had convicted him of allowing offense to grow between him and his children. One of his daughters, the child with whom he had experienced the greatest tension, came on stage. Sincerely and humbly, this father and pastor got down on his knees, produced a wash basin and towel, and washed his daughter's feet. Tears poured down both their faces as he apologized for years of hurt and frustration.

Suddenly wash basins appeared for anyone who wanted one. My dad grabbed a towel and started washing my feet. With tears he then told me what I had needed to hear all those years. He was sorry he had put pressure on me to fulfill the prophecies God had shown him about my life. He said he would never bring them up again. He said he loved me and that he would no longer try to steer me away from the film industry. I tried to stay strong and show no emotion, but inside I felt that deep warmth and peace I had experienced all those years ago when I sang "Holy and Anointed One."

That was what I needed. I was now free to move forward in my calling. But more importantly, I was now free to move forward in my relationship with God.

Part II: My Mom, Just Mom

If the word "complicated" indicates my relationship with my dad growing up, then certainly "simple" would describe the relationship I had with my late mom, Michal Ann Goll. In fact it was not just the relationships that were "complicated" or "simple," but the people themselves. Where my dad's Ezekiel-like visions and prophetic experiences led to difficult, complex questions, stories of Mom's youth had her running in the fields on her family's farm, singing to the Lord. Singing, and singing, and singing. No matter what changes or challenges would come Mom's way during her lifetime, she really never deviated from that simplicity.

Mom was the "steady Eddie" to my dad's quixotic antics. She was calm, cheerful, private, and hard-working. That great, old-school maxim comes to mind: "If you can't say something nice, don't say nothing at all." Well, that was her. No one ever heard her say something not nice! But don't mistake niceness for weakness. This farm and field girl could handle livestock, open jars difficult for men, and knew how to keep four kids in order. But there I'm getting ahead of my story. Let's back up.

Hope Deferred

After seven years of heartbreaking barrenness, my mom and dad had wept and prayed for children to the point where they understood all too well the declaration of Proverbs 13:12: "Hope deferred makes the heart sick." The top fertility specialist in the Midwest had pronounced conception impossible. He had never seen a condition like my mom's. No amount of medicine or procedure would make motherhood a possibility.

They were so heartsick, in fact, that they had a plan B and found themselves at a Lutheran adoption agency in St. Louis. When the agency told my parents that they had been given top placement and were now approved to adopt a certain baby boy, my parents took a walk on the facility grounds and prayed about their decision. After pacing and praying and discussing, Mom and Dad went back inside the building and informed the agency that would yield their right to this boy to the next couple. They still had hope for a God who heard their prayers.

Another year went by, and Mom had not seen any change or heard any more direction from the Lord. "God, I will not like it," Mom quietly but desperately prayed one day, "but I will yield to You my right and desire to be a mother."

At that moment the invisible voice of God filled her: "I appreciate your attitude, but I am not requiring this of you. I say to you, you must *fight for your children.*" The Lord had spoken, and this command unleashed in my mother a warring intercession unlike anything she had experienced. Two years and a couple miraculous healings later, I was born. After all those years, my mom was the happiest woman to ever become a mother.

"Oh, so *you're* the miracle baby?" I've heard that one a lot over the years. Time to set the record straight: Miracles were required for *each* child to be born. After giving birth to me, my mom's body, strange as it may sound, returned to its pre-healed state. Then God healed her again and she gave birth to my sister GraceAnn. The pattern recurred, resulting in my brother Tyler. Every life really is a miracle, but my parents were racking up lots of "special" miracles!

Shaking Things Up

Remember what I said at the beginning about my parents allowing God to change them? Well, something needed to change with Mom and Dad. Even at five years old, I could see that was the case! Mom was absolutely content to hide in Dad's shadow. She would even relate to God *through my dad*. Now, if you're married, hopefully you've experienced that magical but scary moment where God speaks something to you through your spouse. If you haven't, watch out! It's gonna happen. However, my mom took that a little *too* far. God would simply communicate to her through her anointed husband, she thought! Then one day God got tired of waiting and flat out told her, "Look, I want to talk to you Myself!"

By the time baby number three arrived, Dad was done having kids. I imagine him praying to God, "Love the ones I have, thank You very much. But I'm fine. Really."

"But Jim," Mom said one day, "I had a dream about another baby, a baby girl named Rachel." God always told my dad what was up. That was the deal. Either dad would have a dream, or an angel would fly in with a message. And so far, no dreams, no angels. In my dad's mind, no babies were on the way!

Then one day my dad came home from his job at the church and found a sign I had taped to the front door. The sign proclaimed: "It's blue!" Dad was about to discover that *blue* was the color of the positive sign on the pregnancy test Mom had taken that morning. "You can't be pregnant," my dad complained. "God didn't tell me anything!"

"But *I* told you," Mom replied calmly. These incidents marked gradual changes in my parents' marriage. Slowly the two of them became more of a ministry *team*. Little did they know, however, that this was just the beginning of the change.

Strange Visitors

In 1992 on the Day of Atonement, my parents were sound asleep when a lightning bolt struck in our backyard and a blinding light burst into Mom and Dad's bedroom. Suddenly a man stood at the end of my parents' bed. And not just any man. This was an angel, and around him emanated a presence which my mom later described as "the terror of God." Of course, my siblings and I somehow slept through all these fireworks!

What I do recall was having a mom for a few weeks who was in a bit of a permanent daze. The one "visit" had turned into a string of visits over nine weeks. Mom spared us kids most of the details but would simply tell us that an angel had visited her the night before. Later, I found out that God had revealed to both Mom and Dad that

He wanted to visit my mother, alone. Not my dad, not the two of them together—just Mom.

It was a strange season, yet it seemed normal—mundane, even. Mom would get ready for bed early. As evening wore into night, I remember our dog would seem agitated and look up at some invisible *something* on the ceiling. Then the next morning, Mom would seem fine but a little distracted. What I didn't know was that she was experiencing so much of God's power that, after some encounters, Mom would check her own pulse because she didn't know if she was still alive or not!

This all changed the Goll family at the most fundamental level. Dear, gentle, serene Michal Ann was undergoing a personality transplant! Gone were timidity and the fear of man. Suddenly present was a tremendous unspoken authority. It was like we got a new, upgraded mom. Both my parents wrote about the changes and challenges Mom's transformation brought to their marriage.[2] Suddenly, Mom was not so quiet! And sometimes Dad missed the old Michal Ann. But they both agreed that what God was doing was good and that they would allow Him to re-form their relationship.

The Turning Point

Let's return to the year 2000, the turning point when my dad promised that he would never again pressure me about the prophetic words from before my birth. It was like my faith muscle suddenly came alive again. In response to this freedom, I took a break from going to church with my family and started going to church with some friends in a completely different stream of Christianity. (Can I just say that, for most PKs, a season like this is a very good idea?) My faith was becoming my own for the first time.

This new freedom also enabled me to start learning from, dare I say it, my parents! It suddenly felt natural for my mom and me to form a friendship around reading the Bible together. Mom was no theologian like my dad, but she did teach me to *experience* the Bible. She said, "Don't worry about how many pages you read. Read until you are full." I want to devote this next section to my mom because Valentine's Day was her birthday. And it happened that Valentine's Day also became the day I first encountered the Holy Spirit.

Valentine's Day

Aside from my nominal acceptance of Christ at age five, the first time I ever prayed to *Jesus* specifically was in the spring of 2004. That's right. It is totally possible for someone to grow up in the church, surrounded by miracles, prophecies, and angels and not know Jesus. Selah.

Somehow God had absolutely *hoodwinked* this sarcastic, movie-loving PK into attending a ministry school in Pasadena, California. After five months in the school, I began praying to Jesus and asking Him questions. *Immediately* I started seeing prophetic pictures in my mind's eye. This was a weird experience for me because, remember, I had not had a dream from God, had not had any sort of vision from Him, since I was seven years old. I had become convinced that God did not speak to me.

I woke up on February 14, 2004 at 7 A.M. to attend our school's morning prayer meeting. I had been to several of these meetings and not much enjoyed them. What did I know about praying? They were mostly a showcase for the good "prayer people" to strut their stuff. One moment I was sitting there silently. The next moment, to my surprise and everyone else's, I was yelling. "I am not satisfied! I am not satisfied with a half portion of passion. I want a full portion of passion, and anything in me that wants less, cut it off!"

That evening I went to my dorm room. I was sitting down, and a friend came in. We started talking about what we thought heaven would be like. I looked down, and my left foot was twitching. "That's strange," I thought. A few minutes later this twitching spread up my leg and escalated to outright shaking. Word spread to the other seven guys from my dorm, and suddenly my room was full of faces watching me, some understandably laughing. Then the shaking hit me so violently I knocked the chair I was sitting in against the wall and fell to the ground, writhing.

Internally, my mind was scrambling. "What is going on, Jesus?" I thought. "Is this just spectacle?" Then the question from age seven returned: *Does God want to control me?* Still thrashing, and with all my peers around me, I focused on one leg. Could I stop one leg from shaking? The leg steadied. Yes, I could resist this shaking if I wanted to. I could say no. And at that moment, while shaking on the outside, I felt deep peace on the inside. God just wanted to roughhouse with me! And so I let Him.

This encounter with the Holy Spirit lasted for two hours. Eventually a deep groaning came out of my mouth, and I ended up giving a prophetic word to a schoolmate I did not get along with! My classmates in response started interceding for our school and for each other, and then all eight of us entered into the most transparent and joyful time of confession I have ever experienced. I went to bed at 5 A.M. that Valentine's Day, tired, covered in rug burns, and very much a new man.

I told my parents all about it the next morning. Their joy for me soared through the roof. I felt a new emotion then. I think you would call it *pride*. For the first time I was proud to be part of this bizarre Goll family! I was proud that it meant being a person of encounter. And most of all, I was proud that Jesus wanted to know me. Though it took twenty years, my Lord was committed to pursuing me until I was His.

Anyone Can Inherit

My life contains a lot of unique or even sensational elements (angels, miraculous births, etc.) that you may or may not relate to. However, I hope there's something good at the center of my story that *is* relatable—my desire to pass on the blessings of my parents to the next generation. For me these are things like the fear of the Lord, simplicity of worship, hearing God's voice, servanthood, and God's compassionate desire to heal. But in order to pass these bounties on, I must first inherit them for myself.

What's on your list? What do you want to inherit? You may come from a family with lots of spiritual blessings or maybe just a few. That will work fine—Jesus loves to multiply! You may be the first in your family to know the Lord. Perfect—God wants to make you the first of a mighty line! And if it helps, look around for a godly family you admire and ask the Lord to deposit some of their strengths in you. Ultimately, these blessings don't spring from a parent or from any man but come "from above, coming down from the Father of lights" (James 1:17). And I believe God is on pins and needles, waiting to hear what His kids are going to ask Him for next.

Notes

1. Pope John Paul II, "Familiaris Consortio: The Role of the Christian Family in the Modern World," Domestic-Church.com, 2010, Cooperators in the Love of God the Creator, http://www.domestic-church.com/CONTENT.DCC/BASEDOCS/JPII_FC_3.HTM.

2. James W. Goll and Michal Ann Goll, *Angelic Encounters* (Lake Mary, FL: Charisma House, 2007), 25–35.

CHAPTER 4

GREEN GRASS

Yana Banova Brink

From the time I was a small girl, I have been asked the same question over and over again. If I had a nickel for every time I smiled and gave my answer to that very question, I would be rich. It was a question that I did not know how to properly answer. "What is it like to have Georgian and Winnie Banov as your *parents?*"

My honest answer was always the same. I would smile and say, "Normal." Sometimes I could sense that my response was not the answer the person asking the question was looking for, so I would add something extra, "I mean, they are totally amazing, but they are still normal to me." I knew my parents were wonderful, influential, and inspiring people. I knew they did amazing things, and I knew that I was a part of it, but it didn't seem like a big deal. It was simply what we did. It was our life.

I have to assume, however, that "normal" is subjective to each person. Most American babies don't get their passport at two months old and celebrate turning six months old in South Africa, like I did. It never seemed weird that we traveled the globe, preaching the gospel, loving on the poor. Living out of a suitcase, eating in restaurants morning, noon, and night, and homeschooling was our normal. That was my normal, and I loved it.

I should back up and start from the beginning. I was born in Dallas, Texas by emergency caesarean. My mother began to hemorrhage at 7½ months pregnant while my parents were attending a conference. Doctors thought my mother had placenta previa, which meant that her placenta was blocking the birth canal and she would need to have a C-section. When they performed the procedure and I came out colorless, they realized it was actually placenta accreta, which meant my umbilical cord had not been properly attached to the placenta; instead it had attached itself along the wall of the uterus. I was getting my nutrition intravenously through micro-fine connections all the way around the uterus. So when they cut her open, they severed my blood supply and did not know it. I was rushed to the NICU and my mother nearly hemorrhaged to death.

Once we were both stabilized, the doctors told my father that they had only read of this complication in medical journals but never seen it in person. From a medical standpoint, they said I was a miracle baby and I should have been lost shortly after conception. It seemed that God had great plans for me and I was not going to miss out on them. After a miraculously short visit in the NICU, we returned home to Tacoma, Washington where I was raised until the age of 12.

Prior to my birth, my parents met during the height of the Jesus Movement at a Bible college in Texas. They fell in love, were married, and committed themselves to serve the Lord together in a radical way. They traveled the United States preaching the gospel, doing street evangelism, ministering to children with their award-winning albums *Music Machine* and *Bullfrogs and Butterflies*, and later, with their band Silverwind.

After 13 years of legalism and spiritual oppression from their leaders my mom was burned out. She loved God, but was done with religion and did not want anything to do with it anymore. My dad had been trained to put ministry before family, so he would leave her at home and he would go minister alone. I was about two years old when they stopped traveling together. They lived together, but in a way they were divorced in their hearts. She was home working a job at Nordstrom's and he was out on the road, and I grew up in the chasm between them.

As a result, my childhood was split between home and abroad. Half of the time I was home with my mom living a relatively typical life— going to elementary school; playing at parks and museums; spending time with aunts, uncles and cousins; and celebrating birthdays and holidays with our large "family," which was a big group of our blood relatives and close friends. The other half, I traveled with my dad as he ministered at churches and preached the gospel to the nations. When I was nine, I had premier gold status with United Airlines because I had flown more than 25,000 miles in one year alone. We went to Hawaii, where my dad would speak to the students at YWAM. We went to Bulgaria and spent time with orphans. We took road trips all over the great 48 states.

One of my favorite parts of flying somewhere with my dad was the goody bag from my mom. She would pack me a special bag that I could only open after I had boarded the plane. It was my yellow Mickey Mouse duffle bag and it saw many, many airports. To this day it still smells like bubblegum. She would pack crayons and coloring books, stuffed animals, candy, and snacks. My generation did not grow up with iPads and iPhones. We self-entertained and used our imagination. I had flown so much that I memorized the entire United Airlines Safety Information emergency speech and I would recite it loudly in tandem with the flight attendant for all the nearby passengers to hear. When we would visit the YWAM bases in Hawaii, I would find the binder with all the students' pictures. I'd pick out my favorite faces, memorize their names, and I would go seek them out. I had no inhibitions. I would introduce myself and ask them to be my best friend. They would take me under their wing and more often than not I would end up bunking in the girls' dorms the rest of our trip. I absolutely loved traveling with my dad. My time at home with my mom was equally just at fun. I loved my life. My mom was happy when I was with her, and when I was with my dad, he was happy too.

I thought we were a happy family with a good life. I did not know that my parents' marriage was crumbling and that they were headed toward divorce. Ministry burnout and religion had pushed a wedge between them and they were ready to call it quits. I never saw their fights or knew their struggles, however, and I continued to grow up happy. I was spending quality time with my dad as we adventured around the world making beautiful memories, and the rest of the time balanced at home with my mom, friends, and school.

In a way, I was leading a double life—half home, half away. That came to a screeching halt in 1994. There was a supernatural move of God happening in Toronto, Canada. It was an outpouring of the presence of God in a new and exciting way. My parents took a trip to Toronto Airport Christian Fellowship and my mom came back a different person. I knew something had changed when one day my mom forgot to pick me up from school. After waiting for hours I saw her car peel down the road, but it was not my mother driving. It was their secretary, Rebecca. I yelled, "Where have you guys *been?* You *forgot me?*"

Rebecca looked at me and said, "Something has happened to your mom." I was worried, but she told me it was a good thing. I was confused. When I opened the front door I heard my mom laughing, which was not out of the ordinary, however, it was *how* she was laughing. I walked into the kitchen and saw something crazy. My mom was rolling around on the floor, laughing, shrieking, screaming, and crying.

I was confused. *"You left me at school because Mom was laughing?"* She seemed drunk. Which she was—drunk in the Spirit of God. Somehow she got up off the floor and began dancing around the kitchen. Then she took a piece of paper, tore it up, grabbed a jar of confetti, ran into the backyard, and threw them all up into the air, showering the grass below her feet. I didn't understand what was happening. Later I learned that it was a party. It was a celebration. God had wooed her back to Himself and she was His again. She had returned to her first love and this was the dawning of a new age. On that paper was written the names of major cities around the world. As she threw the confetti and torn-up pieces of paper in the air, she was "sowing" seeds of the cities that God would take her to—and ultimately us, as a family.

After that, I saw my mom change more. She was happy, really happy, laughing and crying at the drop of a hat. I remember one time I heard her screaming from the other end of the house. I ran to her room where I found her, stiff as a statue, eyes as wide as plates. She gasped and said, *"He's heeeereeee!"* After a brief moment of terror, assuming that there was an intruder in our house, I realized she was having an open vision of Jesus. I don't know what scared me more— my mom screaming or the thought of Jesus manifesting Himself in my house. Another scary encounter happened one morning when my mom was driving me to school. While we were on a bridge I saw her frantically looking back and forth between the rearview mirror and the side-view mirror. Then she started screaming her head off. I was absolutely freaking out. I was yelling, *"Mom! Pull over! Stop the car!"* but she couldn't because we were still on the bridge. Once we got to the other side she pulled over. After a few minutes she could finally speak. She told me she had seen two angels. One was sitting in the back seat and the other one was hanging outside of the car, flying alongside us, hair blowing in the wind. Her two angels made repeat appearance often. Crazy things were happening.

My mom was not the only one who changed. My dad was different too. He also had an encounter with the Lord and he had changed. Both of them were so happy and in love with the Lord that it manifested a renewal in their marriage. A reawakening. My parents were happy, in love, and loving God together. That made me realize that they weren't happy before. Shortly after that, my life totally changed. My parents decided we would travel as a family. They took me out of school, began to homeschool—or as we affectionately called it, "road school"—sold my childhood home, relocated us to Florida, and began our life of full-time ministry as a reunited family. Things were completely different.

What did my new life look like? We began to spend more time in planes, trains, and hotels than we did at home. We ate more restaurant meals than home cooked. Ministering at churches for extended periods of time—days, weeks, even months! God was moving so powerfully in my dad's meetings that one weekend of revival meetings turned into nine months. I spent my 13th birthday in the Philippines, my 16th birthday in Toronto, my 18th birthday in Mozambique, and my 21st in South Africa. We spent almost every Christmas from 2000 to 2008 in Nicaragua with orphans. Holidays and birthdays were not off limits. It was an exciting, relentless schedule that required a lot of sacrifice. While I never had a high school graduation and I didn't go to prom, I did have unique life experiences. I was comfortable in a room full of strangers; I could make friends anytime, anywhere. I tried to be as open and accessible as possible with everyone I met, which at times left me hurt when others judged me. There was an element of needing to protect myself and not let my guard down *too* much. A challenging part of being in the public eye, being "famous," was that people felt like they knew me and knew my family. The reality was that only a few people knew me on a deep level. I wanted people to know me in a genuine way, but we weren't in one place long enough for that to happen.

I had the privilege of growing up with a broad worldview. Most children in America are shielded from suffering. They do not have the opportunity to see more than their own city. I saw a lot of poverty, pain, despair, and sorrow. That caused me to be tender, aware, sensitive, and have a heightened compassion for others. My compassion for others' suffering was overwhelming at times. When I was 18 we went to Mozambique to visit Heidi and Rolland Baker's orphanage. I sat for hours with a teenage boy who was lame and prayed for his healing. Another time I prayed and wept for a lame Roma (gypsy) woman in Kazanluk, Bulgaria. Once my parents and I were in Ethiopia and a little boy was begging at our taxi window. He was missing a hand, his eyes were sunken in, and his eyelids were hanging down. He was so close to the car that his tears were dripping onto the window. I remember lying on my hotel bed crying out to God, "Why is there so much suffering in the world?" I felt powerless. That moment still makes my heart hurt and brings a lump to my throat.

Not everyone I prayed for received healing, but I'm certain that each person I hugged and cried with experienced the love of God in a tangible way. While I have felt immense sorrow and empathy for others, I've also experienced incredible joy. I saw a blind Mozambican woman receive her sight. I saw two deaf and mute boys hear and talk for the first time. I have danced with Bulgarian Roma (gypsies) in the rain. I have given orphans toys on Christmas. I remember an adorable Mozambican orphan girl named Paulina wandering into my room. She must've been about three years old. I shared my Starburst candies with her and her eyes lit up like stars. That was a precious moment. It was that same morning that I woke up to the sound of African women singing and praising God outside my window. I will never forget the sound of their voices. I've seen Mama Heidi Baker sit down in the garbage dump dirt with her "children" and hold them, pray for them, and eat an offering of cashews one of them had found in the trash and given to her. She was an inspiration to me then, and still is now. So many beautiful moments of joy and pain are etched into my memory and ingrained on my heart. I believe that the extreme joys and pains I have felt for others have made me a very compassionate and empathetic person.

Throughout those years of relentless full-time ministry, there were moments where I wanted something different. A more "normal" normal, where I didn't have to live on planes, trains, and automobiles.

Where I could make friends and keep them for more than a day, and where I didn't feel sacrificed for the sake of the "ministry." As a teenager, missing my home church's youth retreats, celebrating birthdays in a foreign country without my friends, and wishing that holidays could be spent with our family back in Washington was very hard. There I was, blessed beyond measure, with more unique life experiences than many adults, yet I felt that I was missing something, and that little something was balance.

I was 18 when I approached my parents with the idea of not traveling with them anymore. They thought I was crazy, but they agreed. I got a job at a clothing store, went to youth group, sang on the worship team, and lived at home by myself while my family was gone. The grass is definitely greener on the other side, and I quickly realized my idea wasn't as great as I had thought it would be, but my pride didn't want to admit that to my parents. (How often are our greatest strengths our greatest weaknesses?)

Instead of going back on the road I decided to try my hand at college. That first year was very challenging. More than just typical freshman jitters, this was the most outside of my comfort zone that I had ever been. For the first time in my life I found myself surrounded by people who didn't believe what I believed at all, some who did, and everywhere in between. This was my first real step into the world, outside of my Christian bubble and away from my parents. This was my chance to see who I was raised to be and what I was made of. But I wasn't sure how to do that. Did I need to be really zealous for God? Did I need to read my Bible outside on the grass for everyone to see? Did I need to get up on the table at lunch and preach Jonathan Edwards' "Sinners in the Hands of an Angry God"? Did I need to wait up for my roommates to get home from partying so I could tell them I was praying for them and God loved them?

I was concerned that if I wasn't obviously, overtly, and proactively "Christian," then they might not know; they wouldn't see who I was. I wanted so badly to represent who I was and who God was that I tried too hard. It was a rocky learning curve. I didn't know that just being myself, loving God, and operating out of that love was all I needed to do.

Another thing I learned—English Literature bores me, and I'm even worse at Algebra. Oh, but the arts! That's what made my heart tick. Armed with the knowledge that academics were not my strong suit, I switched gears. I heard about a small ministry school with an emphasis on music and art in Croydon, England. I found my bags packed again and headed across the pond. During my four months there I made deep friendships with my 12 schoolmates. It was a pressure cooker. We lived together, played music, sang, cried, laughed, learned about the Lord, and challenged each other. It was real community. For the first time in my life I opened up my heart and was truly vulnerable and transparent with my friends and leaders. When they responded with love and acceptance, it changed me. I was set free from the fear of rejection. There were no expectations put on me and I was not afraid to be myself. It was evident to me that the students and leaders alike were a demonstration of God's great love.

My time in England was an amazing season. I highly recommend ministry school to all young people. When that was over, I moved back home with my parents. I had come full circle. I went from traveling full time with my parents, left home, gone to schools, and then moved back. They welcomed me with open arms and offered me a position on their staff to be their missions coordinator. I would plan the trips with my parents and help the groups get their tickets, passports, hotels, and travel details sorted out. It was a perfect scenario for me because I finally had balance for both—ministry and the stability of planting roots and being grounded somewhere safe. I had time to invest in my friendships at our new home church in Harrisburg, Pennsylvania, and twice a year I would travel overseas with the missions group to Bulgaria, Greece, Turkey, Romania, and Nicaragua. It was a win-win. I absolutely love short-term missions trips. They are the perfect opportunity to see the Lord in action, to give to the poor, and even to fall in love. Yes, I fell in love with my husband on the mission field.

One perk of traveling the world—meeting boys. Even a minister's daughter has a one-track mind. I had met my fair share of great guys, but none of them captured my attention. I knew what I wanted, and my standards were high. So when Chris, my friend's younger brother, approached me on a missions trip to Turkey and confessed that he had liked me since he was 16, I was shocked. I was flattered, but shocked. We had known his family for years. His parents were pastors and we had been to their church countless times, his sister and I had been good friends for many years, and I had known Chris since he was 13—barely old enough to see his head over the drum set on stage! Because of that, I had never pictured him that way. In my mind, he was young and kind of dorky! I told him that we should just be friends, and it broke his heart. He told his parents, "If Yana is not God's will for me then I don't know *what* is!"

We didn't talk much until a year later on another missions trip. When I saw him again he was so different. He had changed, matured, and his heart for the Lord was so apparent, but I still wasn't giving him an inch. He had to win me over. We had another talk and he told me that he still liked me and that he would continue to pursue me. He was persistent. He wouldn't take no for an answer, and I am so glad he didn't. We began to email each other a few times a week. After four months of emailing we had become great friends. I realized he was everything I had ever wanted and more. He asked to court me and a week into being official I knew I had found the one. This is who I would marry.

For the first time in my life, I opened up my heart to love and I fell head over heels for Chris. We dated long distance from Pennsylvania to Maine for nine months. On the same missions trip that we fell in love on, a year later, Chris stashed an engagement ring in his suitcase. On our day off Chris took me to our favorite coffee shop in Istanbul near the Blue Mosque and he proposed. After my shock wore off and I exclaimed "*Yes!*" we were interrupted mid-kiss by our waiter. Apparently, PDA is not allowed within a certain radius of mosques!

A year later, in June 2008, we were married in a small park with 29 of our closest family and friends surrounding us. Even the scorching 98-degree weather couldn't put a damper on our beautiful day. I was a blushing bride, and quite nearly a sweaty one! We quickly settled into married life, but not before tackling a total home renovation. A few months after we moved in, we found out that we were pregnant with our first baby. It was sooner than we had planned to start a family, but we were equally excited and scared out of our minds to become parents. Our son Ruehl Grayson was peacefully born at home and changed our lives. Two years later, with another home birth, we welcomed our daughter Amelie Fiora. Our family grew leaps and bounds, as did our hearts. Christopher and our children have enriched my life deeply and given me a new stability and purpose.

So now I find myself in a very new season—motherhood. And just like I did in college, I am learning to navigate my way through this season, but this time with more grace and understanding. I'm learning consistency, contentment, and purpose in who I am and what I do. When people ask me what I do, I say, "I'm a SAHM—stay-at-home mom," but really, what I mean to say is, "I am a loving, hard-working, rockin' mom, dedicated and committed to raising my children in truth, with the understanding that we are God's love in action."

I, like many other ministers' kids, spent my life *doing* ministry and I wouldn't trade it for the world. But when the *doing* part stopped, I was thrown off balance. I had to learn how to let my life *be* my ministry. Coming from the family that I do, I definitely struggled with wondering what my parents and others would think if I didn't continue in their footsteps and commit my life to full-time ministry. Instead of judging me, my parents blessed my decision to be a wife, mother, and artist. I've spent the last few years establishing a new normal and I have learned something very valuable. Even though I don't want to be an evangelist like my father or a teacher like my mother, I still have a very valid place to minister from—as a mother, a friend, a wife, an artist. I have chosen a different life for myself. I honor and respect people who have given their lives to full-time ministry. It is a high calling that only God can place on one's life. My parents still serve the Lord full time and they love it. For the rest of us who have chosen careers and parenthood—wherever you are, whatever you are doing, it *is* ministry as long as your heart is submitted to God.

The definition of a Christian is to bear Christ. We are His body and wherever we go, whomever we talk to, we are Christ to them. We can all believe for the supernatural realm of heaven to manifest in our lives. We can pray for our friends, co-workers, and neighbors and see them blessed. We can pray for the sick and see them healed. We can give to the needy and homeless. We can go on short-term missions trips and bring God's love and joy to the poor. I plan to take my children to the garbage dumps with my parents' ministry as often as possible so that they too can have life-changing and character-molding experiences similar to what I had.

The mindset that you are either in ministry or in the world inhibits us from reaching our full potential to bear fruit for the Kingdom. Don't put yourself in that silly box. The two don't have to be separate! It is my desire to raise my children with that mindset as their normal—that we are *all* ministers of the gospel and can demonstrate the love of Christ to everyone we come into contact with. So now, my "normal" might be more relatable to others—less gallivanting around the globe and more sleepless nights, finger-painting, playing at the park, and eating Cheerios. Do I miss my parents and our adventures? I certainly do, but every day God teaches me that this is exactly where He wants me to be, and I am learning to embrace it all. My grass is green.

CHAPTER 5

ALL IN THE FAMILY

Lori Arnott Lawlor

I Met Jesus

I remember the day that I met Jesus. I was sitting on my parents' bed, and my dad was explaining to me who Jesus was, that He loved me. He explained to my little heart that I needed a savior who had paid for everything I would ever do wrong, and if I believed in Him I would live forever in heaven with Him. I was three years old, and to this day I can still feel the impact of that decision in my heart. I choose Jesus again!

Now that I'm 50 (and hopefully wiser), I have begun to appreciate that salvation experience that was birthed in the love of God—for me first, and then back to Him. It's part of my bedrock. I was not scared into meeting Jesus, but rather "loved" into meeting Him. Through the years, with decisions made, both good and bad, I have been deeply aware of how Jesus feels about my choices. I've been aware of hurting

Him or pleasing Him with my decisions, without condemnation, but aware of His preferences.

I can honestly say that there has never ever been a day in my life when I have regretted the decision I made at three to welcome Jesus into my heart and life.

Dad the Teacher

When I was little, my dad would read me Bible stories—his way. What I mean is, he never read me a Bible story from a children's book (you know, the ones with pictures), but rather always read me Bible stories right from the Bible. He has always had a way of reading the Bible and making it come alive. Those of us who know him and have heard him speak know he has a way of reading the Scriptures so naturally. He always wanted me to hear it "without interpretation" and as truthfully as possible. I now understand that it is a part of who he is—wanting to keep things honest and true, without embellishment and man's interference. He has taught me by example to expect the real thing from God. My model and hunger to ask lots of questions began with these encounters. He would encourage me, "If you want to know more about something, ask." Sometimes, after I had asked many questions in a row, he would say, "Wait till the end, and I will answer them all."

Learning to ask questions of others, but especially with the Lord, is still such a valuable tool for me. In our story times, I would love to hear about Jesus—His kindness, His wise responses. He was so clever!

As a little girl, I loved to picture what my ears were hearing. The book of Revelation became such living pictures for me all through life—the place we were going. Heaven. It was easy for me to visualize the streets made of real gold! It was easy for me to anchor my hope in this place of beautiful gemstones and peaceful rivers and gardens. These embedded memories would play a significant role in my life many years later.

My dad is still my favorite speaker and teacher. No matter how often I've heard him speak the same messages (some of them dozens of times), I love to hear him share them again. I still love the way he thinks, questions, and explains.

Dad the Adventurer

My dad was born on December 25, 1940, John Goodwin Arnott. His middle name, Goodwin, is to honor the name of the doctor who delivered him and probably saved his life at birth, as the umbilical cord was wrapped twice around his neck. I am told that when he was a little boy, he needed braces on his legs in order to walk, as his ankles were weak and needed support. I remember when I was little, although he took us ice skating, he did not skate with us because his ankles were weak.

He has always been adventurous, jumping on the bread wagon and the milk wagon that would pass on his street—at three years of age! He has always wanted to go! His mom would tie him to the tree in the front yard and neighbors passing by would hear his plea, "Please undone me." It's wonderful to see, with all of the world traveling he does now, that it has always been something he is wired for and happy to do.

I must admit that this "adventure bug" of his hasn't always felt great to me. We moved every couple of years and didn't like it as little girls. Although my dad is now recognized as an amazing visionary, I didn't see it that way as I was growing up. As I mentioned, we moved often, and they were usually significant moves—from the big city to a farm! We moved from one country to another. (Only to Florida, but having moved from Canada, the other kids thought I had lived in an igloo!) We never moved just down the street. It was always a whole new environment.

My Responsibilities

I am the oldest of two girls. Vicki, my sister, is two years younger. One of the things my heavenly Father has restored and healed in my heart is some of the heartache and fear from these big changes— different homes, different schools, different friends, etc. As the oldest, of course, my mom and dad would ask me to take care of my little sister. On one hand, it was great to learn about responsibility and feel so trusted by my parents—all a good part of my training in caring for others, motherhood, church leadership, etc. However, at the same time, my heart was also hearing and believing some wrong messages about being "responsible for everyone and everything!"

I wanted to be a good girl. I wanted to please my parents. It mattered to me when my dad was upset with me. I'm thankful they taught me right from wrong. Usually we would wait in our room for

Dad to come in and discipline us. Honestly, I think the wait was worse than the punishment, knowing I had disappointed Mom or Dad. I really wanted to be a good girl, but again, my heart began to believe untruths about love.

Holy Spirit Encounter

As mentioned before, I have been a Christian for most of my life. If ever I compared myself to others, who perhaps had more dramatic salvation testimonies, my dad would say to me, "Honey, you have the greatest testimony of all—the saving, keeping, grace of God for all of your life!" He exposed me to some wonderful giants of faith, such as Kathryn Kuhlman, and for that I feel really privileged. I've heard great Bible teachers, been in wonderful corporate worship services, been involved in deliverance ministry, small groups in our home, and even helping in the crèche when Benny Hinn's ministry first began in Toronto. My hunger for more of God has always been nurtured and encouraged, primarily by my dad. When I was 11, I began to hear about the baptism of the Holy Spirit, and a desire to know Him and be filled with Him began to stir in my heart. For at least one year, I went up for every altar call given to receive this baptism. I remember feeling discouraged and disappointed that it never happened to me!

One night while living in Florida, my mom and dad took me to Jamie Buckingham's church for the evening service. We often went there on Sunday nights after attending our local Baptist church on Sunday mornings. Our local church had wonderful programs for kids, but not too much freedom in the Holy Spirit. In those days, the doctrine taught there was that speaking in tongues was of the devil.

Meanwhile, my heart was longing for this experience and to know Him more. During this evening service, visiting speakers Charles and Frances Hunter were there. Again, like most Charismatic meetings in the '70s, there was an altar call to be baptized in the Holy Spirit. Because of my discouragement and disappointment on this already, I had decided that I would never go up again for one of these altar calls. God knew where I was, that I wanted Him, and He could find me!

To this day, I do not know how I got to the front. I found myself there, speaking in tongues! I loved my friends and youth group at our Baptist church. I really wanted to share with them my excitement about what God had just done for me, just shown me. I did not know how to explain it all to them. I didn't know how to argue the theology with them. My dad gave me some advice that day, which has proven to be pure wisdom, and I believe carried him, too, through stewarding the amazing work of God he has led and is leading. He said to me, "Honey, you don't have to explain everything to them; just tell them what happened to you." It has been the "testing of the fruit" example that is so valid and relevant all over the world now.

Sad Time

My parents separated and then divorced when I was 15 and 16. It was obviously a very sad time. I came back to Toronto with my dad, and my sister stayed in Florida with my mom. Although it was such a sad time and our family was torn in two, it was also a treasured time between my dad and I. We had each other. We started again, together—new apartment, borrowed furniture, then eventually new furniture!

When he wanted to get married again, he included me. I felt so welcomed into that decision—even helping him pick out her engagement ring! I had known and loved Carol before we moved to Florida. She lived across the street with her two little boys, Rob and Mike, who I sometimes babysat. It was great knowing and loving her (and Rob and Mike) before we became family.

Toronto!

On January 20, 1994, a divine, supernatural visitation from Heaven—the Father's love being poured out sovereignly to all—happened at my dad's church in Toronto. The "Father's Blessing" movement began a fresh revelation for me (and obviously millions of others). This has, of course, always been what Father God has been revealing about Himself, but not always getting through. His heart being revealed to the children, so that our hearts can respond back to Him—all in very personal ways and experiences that we have each had with Him.

I came to Toronto a few days after it all began (I was living in Texas at the time). My dad had called and told me what was happening. Because he had always pursued authentic experiences with God, I never doubted his words when he said to me, "This is the revival I've prayed for all my life!" Throughout the past 20 years particularly, God has been revealing to me just how much I am unconditionally loved. Many of these things were reminders of truths. Many were messages that my dad had tried to teach me throughout my life, but many were fresh pictures and revelations of who my (heavenly) Father really is. In any places my heart had picked up wrong messages, I have been forever changed. The Father's wonderful grace message is continually being poured out into my heart.

Unconditional Love

The Father really loves me! No matter what! If I do everything wrong, from now until Jesus returns, He won't love me any less! If I do everything right, He won't love me more!

My dad used to often hug me and say, "I'm so proud of you; you've never caused me a moment's grief." Obviously, that's not really true, but how wonderful for that to be the predominate thought he has toward me. Unfortunately, sometimes what I heard was, *What happens if I get it wrong? What if I do cause him grief?* The revelation of the Father's unconditional love has been incredibly freeing for me.

I have met many children of pastors and leaders who have grown up in this horrible performance lie. Often when we have grown up believing this, there are unfortunate patterns and reputations that follow us. Sometimes we hide our sin, rebel against God with a vengeance, walk in great fear, but worst of all, we don't step into our inheritance of freedom and destiny, prepared by our family gone before us. This lie can keep us from even greater exploits in God.

Me and Dad

I'm sure most of the other authors and contributors to this book would say that their mothers or fathers were their spiritual parents as well as their natural parents. This is definitely true for me, and I consider it a huge privilege! My dad has exemplified so much to me, including having fun in life and ministry, not taking things too seriously, valuing God's anointing above all else, and so much more. Although both of us are so proud of each other, that does not mean that these two simultaneous relationships have always been an easy journey for my dad and me.

For much of my life, my dad was working, but always had other ministry endeavors he was involved in. I don't remember him at many school performances, and even fewer when my children were growing up. Time with him was a huge thing to contend for (once I figured out that missing that time with him was so important to me). There seemed to always be something or someone more important. My wants or needs felt less urgent, maybe even less significant.

My dad became my dad when he was 21. He was young and as he would say, "Really didn't know too much about being a good dad." His own father was an alcoholic who left them for another family when he was a teenager. Prior to that, his father was "the drunk" his friends teased him about. When his father later came back to God, he repented to his family, and he endeavored to live his remaining days for God and in God.

We all have sad stories—of what we missed out on, of what was abusive, etc. My dad's childhood was no different. But of course, I didn't know how to process this information as a child. I know more now of course. I know now how to put hurts done to me in perspective— how to rationalize and understand harm or neglect done to me in a much more balanced, maybe even distant, less hurtful way. As a child,

I only felt the lack or pain, like we all do. I have been involved (as a participant as well as leading) in various inner-healing ministries for over 30 years, including now, as a trainer for Bethel Sozo here in the UK. I now understand that brokenness produces more brokenness in our own children and others. I now understand that in order for me to "be presented without spot or wrinkle" I will have to embrace the process of my heart's wounds being healed. As mentioned though, any places where others didn't accurately represent God's best for me, I got some bruises and scars along the way. I've also caused some. I don't want any of my brokenness to affect my children or others, especially not out of stubbornness. It's my responsibility to choose life.

Time with Dad

As mentioned, one of the things that I have missed out on was time with my dad. When I was little he worked, then went to Bible school. Although not in full-time ministry until I was an adult, he was always ministering to others, either evangelizing or home groups. When you grow up with deficits on the inside, you aren't always aware of how things have affected you. I remember a time when I was working in Toronto at the Airport Christian Fellowship in the busiest years of the Renewal. I needed to ask my dad a work-related question. I came to his office door upstairs, which was open. He was talking with his friend (and mine) Bill Prankard. I stuck my head in and when I realized he was busy, apologized and said I would come back. Bill had no idea what he said, I don't think, but he said, "No, Lori, come in. You are much more important. My conversation can wait." I can't ever remember anyone honoring me like that before—never as it related to ministry. Maybe it's only how I perceived things, but "the ministry" was almost like God

Himself. How could I ever be hurt that God's needs or conversations were more important than mine?

Let me say here that I don't believe it has ever been intentional with my family to prioritize ministry life over family life. I think one of the biggest challenges for any of us in ministry is to remember to watch for and protect this precious gift of our family. It is not just the attending of special events like birthdays, school pageants, dance recitals, competitions etc., but also just the hanging out time. In my experience now as a pastor, I have found my three children—all adults now, serving in various roles with me here in our church in England— to be my greatest supporters. They have watched folks come and go, and felt the pain of that themselves, yet so supported me. Regarding faithfulness to serve and show up, they are the most faithful.

I personally believe that one of the enemy's agendas throughout history has been to stop the accelerated, exponential blessing of God that goes from one generation to the next. I remember reading years ago that Mrs. Wesley used to spend one hour with each of her children, on their own with her, each week. With my youngest daughter, who is married, we still spend most Tuesday nights together as our "date night." The other two are living back at home at the moment due to career changes, so we see each other most days and plan coffees or breakfasts together. I have experienced the blessing to me from my down line (children), as well as my up line (parents), and I know the power, support, and blessing in that.

In our family quest to fix the broken places and bless more the already good places, we have had lots of conversations and planned quality time together. It's not easy living in different countries, but we have all made effort and paid the necessary costs. A few Christmases ago, my dad phoned and asked if he, Carol, and one my stepbrothers, Mike, could all come for Christmas. It was cramped (I only have three bedrooms) with eight of us for ten days! It was such a wonderful time— sitting around in pajamas together, going out to a concert together, Christmas morning together, playing lots of board games together, with *so* much laughing and simply getting to know each other more! I am so thankful to be living in a family that is determined to not remain stuck in the hurt, offended, distant places with each other.

Worship

My greatest fan when I am leading worship is my dad. I am his favorite worship leader! He has always encouraged me! Of course he and my mom paid for piano lessons, but even in the early days of singing solos in churches, he would say, "Honey, ask the Holy Spirit which song He wants you to sing." As a young teenager, he taught me that some songs were anointed; find those ones. To this day, when I am leading worship, I still ask the Holy Spirit, "Which songs would You like today?" I'm not primarily interested in smooth key changes between songs or singing the current favorites. For me, it's about Him, the Lord; if He doesn't show up for worship, I am really not interested.

I know there were seeds planted in me when I was too little to read and would need my dad to turn the hymnal right way up as I was singing in church. The seeds to love Jesus. The seeds of recognizing the anointing in Kathryn Kuhlman meetings, when Dad would turn to me, tears in his own eyes, and say, "Honey, can you feel that? It's the Holy Spirit's presence." The seeds of encouragement when I would lead worship. The phone calls and texts from Carol (my number-two fan) saying she loved the live CD I produced from a big conference here in England, but that the only problem was, not enough of me! The *always* words of, "*Wow* honey, that was awesome!" when I sat down from leading worship.

I know that I have been given some treasure regarding worship—to look for Him until His Presence comes. Where He is, miracles happen. That's where the bar is set for me.

My Ministry?

I went with my dad on an outreach trip to Mexico a number of years ago. He had been invited to speak. At the end of that trip, the regional superintendent of that group of churches came to him and asked if he (my dad) would please come back next year and address their network of churches that met together annually. My dad said to him, "I'm sorry, but I am not available that week to come as I already have commitments," and turning to me, said to him, "Why don't you invite my daughter, Lori, to come and preach?" Such an awkward moment! What could the man say? What could I say?

As it turned out, he did follow through and ask me to come and address this conference of their network of churches throughout Mexico. I took a team with me and we had a wonderful time. God did amazing things! I fell in love with those people. I was invited back the following year, and during that trip my heart would change forever! I had always made a vow that I would not ever be in full-time ministry.

I was happy to do the occasional trip, happy to minister at home on various teams, but not permanent or, as I have said, full time.

During one of the nights of that conference, there was a call for ministers who wanted more. I knew I wanted to go up for this. I will never, ever forget what happened to me. I was on the floor in a full vision (before I had heard anyone speak of one really, and didn't know what was happening). This is what happened: I was part of a long line of people, longer than I could see the ends of. We were pulling in nets—nets full of souls. We were all working so hard. I was aware that physically I was pulling and my arms were tired. Aware of my physical tiredness, I asked the Lord, "Can I stop yet?"

He said to me, "Not yet, there is more."

We would pull in more nets full of souls, *so* full. Again I asked the Lord, "Can I stop yet?"

He said again, "Not yet, there is more." I knew I was part of the harvest, and like the book of Joel says, those of us pulling nets were all together.

When we had finished, the Lord took me *up*. As I had learned and was natural for me, I asked Him, "Where are we going Lord?"

He said to me, "I am taking you to your reward!" I had always longed for that—I still do long for the day when I will see Him.

He took me into a room, and I just knew somehow that this was the throne room itself. I had expectations as I went in that I would see all of the gemstones and gold I had pictured as a little girl. I thought there would be a lavishly set table prepared for the great wedding feast with every imaginable luxury. I was overwhelmed by what I saw! The room was totally empty except for one thing—Him! He was the only thing in the room. He said to me, "I AM your reward." I was overwhelmed by absolute love and the revelation that He is enough!

We went from there for some wonderful lingering walks—no time restraints, no one else waiting, no one more important. He showed me, just off the throne room, one of my playrooms from a particularly lonely time as a child. I saw all my specific toys in there that I hadn't seen in years. As I looked in from the doorway, I did not want to enter. I did not want to revisit that pain. He said to me, "But you don't understand. I played with you in here. When you thought you were so alone, I was here. This is such a precious room to Me." My heart was healed.

I then asked Him if we could go back to the throne room. I wanted to see it again. Again, only Him! I asked the Lord, "Was this amazing revelation just for me, or for others too?"

He said to me, "Go and tell them—I am their reward, it's all about Me."

I had never wanted "ministry" and all that this word had come to mean. Now it was all different. It wasn't about others. It wasn't about the different measuring sticks of success or, for that matter, failure. It wasn't about pleasing them. It wasn't about being afraid of them. It was about Him! From that moment on, I have been profoundly changed from the inside out. I decided that day I would do whatever He asked of me—even full-time ministry.

Restoration

As a pastor for almost 14 years now, a parent for over 30, and a daughter for 50, I have come to believe that we all have sad stories. We are all heroes for surviving. It's more about whether we take those stories and choose life, choose God in them. It's more about whether we are willing to forgive the wrongs done to us, more about taking responsibility and repenting for the wrongs we do to others. It's more about relationship than anything else.

In my family—and I believe in all families, really—there has been a war. We are all casualties to some extent. Our family—my dad, Carol, myself, siblings, our children—a few years ago all came to the same place; we wanted our family fully restored. In many ways, and for many reasons, we had some significant places of distance. Now all adults, we began to take responsibility for improving our relationships with each other. In our case as a family, there was divorce—my parents, but also my own—which affected relationships. There was distance, living in four different countries. There was also "the ministry" leaving little time for normal family stuff. We don't very often just get to hang out together. We all have busy lives, some of us in ministry, other people wanting our time, etc. (When Jackie, my youngest, got married almost three years ago, for instance, I know Carol wanted to be so much more involved with all the pre-planning stuff, but sadly, was busy traveling with ministry.)

Our family—as individuals, but also as a unit—has definitely paid a price for the last 20 years, especially, of worldwide ministry. We now try to plan more family events—schedule in, because we want to, time with each other. God's work is so important—whether our mission field is church leading, conferences, feeding the poor, school teaching, or secular jobs—but so is our family, the ones He first wants us to bless.

My Father's Blessing

One of the things that I *so* respect my dad for—I can't even say how much—is his willingness to continue to improve the relationship issues that have needed it, even now, with us, with me. More than anyone I know, he endeavors to live what he preaches. Declaring and imparting the Father's blessing is such a wonderful and powerful anointing on his life, obviously affecting millions, but it has also affected me. Dad's 70th birthday party earmarked this event for me, for all of us. He flew us all home (Toronto) for Christmas and his birthday. For each of us present, he went around the table, eldest to youngest, and blessed us, endorsing and blessing our strengths and callings. He told each of us how much he loved us and how proud he was.

My dad has received the Father's blessing in his own heart and then chose to pass on his blessing to us. He could have just received, put it into more sermon notes, and stopped. He has never done that. It has undoubtedly been for the nations, but even more so for us!

Love and Family

The one who is Love Himself lives in each member of my family. First, just for me, I know how much I am loved, so that when I look in Jesus' eyes, I know I am His favorite! Second, He has put each of us in our family in this amazing "inner circle" supportive group of fans for us to be supported and know unconditional love. Third, this "working model" of laughter, forgiveness, offense mending, anger, emotion, and commitment affects our world around us—and affects nations!

I am eternally grateful for my family—my dad, my mom, Carol, my sister and stepbrothers, my ex-husband, my children, my nephews and nieces, and my two grandchildren waiting in Heaven. Each one has been a gift from God to me—yes, sometimes for my character development, to practice forgiveness and also to practice repentance. More than that, though, it's a group of people who are "mine," tied to each other for eternity. They are God's gift to me, to daily show me— through audible words and arms of care—that He is forever loving!

CHAPTER 6

MOVING AHN

Mary Ahn, M.P.P

"To love another person is to see the face of God."
—Victor Hugo, Les Miserables

"Oh no, please go easy on me," were the first words that came out of my father's mouth when I told him that I would be writing a chapter in this exciting book. My response, as I walked away laughing, was simply, "I can't promise anything." The truth is I can't promise that I won't share the good, the bad, and the "not even a mother could love" ugly regarding my experience being the daughter of Pastor(s) Che and Sue Ahn. However, I can testify that those trials and tribulations that my family and I personally adventured through brought me closer to Jesus than I could ever imagine.

I'm sure that my dad's nervous reaction to me writing this chapter stems from the fact that I am notorious for speaking my mind at a moment's notice. Then too, my relationship with my father, according to my personal diagnosis, has not always been a "fantastic" one. In fact, if someone would have asked me ten years ago to sum up our relationship, my response would have been any of the following—bleak, depressing, or (my personal favorite) dismal.

Like Father, Like Son

In retrospect, I now realize my relationship with my father wasn't all that afflictive. There are certainly far worse parent-child relationships out there. For instance, my father and his father (my *harabeoji*) had a very strained relationship while my father was growing up. One story that we children often heard was of a time when my dad and his mother (my grandma or *halmeoni*) lived in Korea while my grandfather (*harabeoji*) got settled in the States. My father didn't see his father for the first five years of his childhood, and when they finally did reunite as a family, life was rocky. Often, my aunt raised my dad as both his parents worked hard to make ends meet. He was a latchkey kid who became involuntarily independent at a young age.

I don't doubt that my grandparents loved their children. However, my *harabeoji* showed his love primarily through provision and discipline. My dad tells the story of his childhood in his book *Fire Evangelism* and describes how, out of anger and frustration, my *harabeoji* would physically discipline my father. My dad was a strong-willed kid and gave my grandparents hell. But there were times where my *harabeoji's* discipline turned into physical abuse, and my dad's relationship with his father was emotionally broken as a result. My father never received affirming words from his dad such as, "I'm proud of you," "You are a great son," or a simple, "I love you." It wasn't until my dad was 40 years old that his father said these simple yet profound words of love for the first time.

I am happy to report that my *harabeoji's* and my father's relationship was completely healed, restored, and renewed. When the renewal movement hit our family and church, my father repented to my *harabeoji* for all his years of rebellion, hurt, and anger he harbored against him. In turn, my *harabeoji* repented for his way of raising my father with such a heavy hand of anger. From that point on, both my father and my *harabeoji* were closer than ever. Being a fellow pastor himself, my *harabeoji* would minister together with my father. It was as if God was reaffirming their father-son relationship in a greater way by establishing it in love and mercy as they shared their ministry.

The healing that took place between my *harabeoji* and my dad overflowed far beyond their individual personal relationship, touching all of our family. My *harabeoji* became an endlessly affectionate and caring man. Whenever we saw him, whether it was in Fairfax, Virginia where he lived or in Los Angeles, he would tell us grandchildren how much he loved us and how proud he was of us. Later, when I went to Regent University in Virginia Beach to study political science in 2005, I would often visit him, and he would eagerly drive me in his Lincoln Continental, better known as "the boat on wheels" with the personalized "Ahn" license plate. I typically wouldn't mind showing off our last name if my grandpa wasn't such "colorful" driver. Given that he was, I was afraid that someone would look up the last name "Ahn" and sue us for reckless driving...and that would be the end to my college fund. He always took me to the same, sometimes questionable, buffet seafood restaurant down the street—Peter Pan. Even though the experience wasn't like the dimming memories of a visit to Neverland, my *harabeoji* always captured our special times with photographs that I still keep to this day. He was indeed a changed man who loved and wasn't afraid to show it. In my personal history he will go down as being the most generous individual I ever knew. When I think of the way my father and grandfather's relationship was healed, it is just another reminder of the miracle-working love of God. Truly, nothing is too big for our Maker!

When It First Began

When I was growing up, I only saw my dad at night after he got back from Fuller Seminary. He was largely unavailable, and sometimes a stranger to me, in that he studied for his Master's and Doctoral degrees back to back. My parents did make a point to have individual dates with each of us four kids. I remember when I had breakfast dates with my dad it was always somewhat uncomfortable. It never felt natural for me to be alone with him. He was always kind and tried earnestly to make me feel special. If I wanted pancakes he would buy me pancakes. If I wanted to play tic-tac-toe at the table, we would play and of course he would let me win. Still, my times with my dad never felt completely intimate. I now believe that as a young child I picked up on the insecurities that my father faced, as he was hurting over his relationship with his father. Because he never experienced affection and love as a child, it was challenging for him to engage in intimacy with us.

My distorted relationship with my father and the subsequent healing of our relationship mirrors my relationship and healing with my heavenly Father. My testimony starts right when I gave my heart to Jesus. I couldn't have been older than five years of age when I gave my life to Jesus. Prior to my conversion I was immersed in every conservative "Christianese" activity. From dance to mime, I was there. I remember when my sisters, Grace and Joy, and I were enrolled in tambourine worship circle, and how we practiced day and night for our Sunday recitals. This life of constant Christian immersion was the only world I knew. My brother, sisters (Gabriel, Grace, Joy), and I had nightly devotions with my parents. They taught us to thank God in our prayers before making our requests.

It was during one of our family devotion times that my dad asked me if I was ready to give my heart to God. I distinctly remember the anticipation that I felt when my father led me through the sinner's prayer. I fully understood what I was doing—that I was finally asking Jesus to come into my heart and for Him to be my Lord and Savior. Little did I know at that young age that my commitment to Jesus and my walk with Christ would be challenged in astronomical ways throughout the next 15 years!

The very next day my father baptized me in our oversized, backyard jacuzzi. Up until that day I knew the jacuzzi as our underwater tearoom where my dad and two sisters would sink to the bottom, and he would serve us proper tea. It's funny the effect daughters can have on fathers. My father would become a different person—a rather British host who had the best underwater tea parties!

In one way, the process of baptism was so familiar to me as I had witnessed many baptisms. Often on summer days my siblings and I played PK games like pretending to baptize each other, and we argued about who would be the pastor and who would get baptized. On that warm Sunday afternoon, I knew this was no game. I was getting baptized in front of my family and family friends. That day the jacuzzi became a sacred space, functioning as a baptismal. Because I wasn't tall enough to reach the bottom, my father sat me on his knee, and led me through the baptism questions. I nervously shared in front of the small audience what Jesus meant to me and why I wanted to be baptized. My response was pure and honest, innocent and true to my five-year-old heart as I shared it. My relationship with Jesus was simple then, without questions, drama, or strife. "Mary Christine Ahn, I baptize you in the name of the Father, Son, and Holy Spirit," were the last words I heard my father speak before I was fully submerged in the water. I went into the water and came up to approving cheers and "Praise God." If I had only known what the future years would hold in store for me, I would have stayed under that water and had endless underwater tea parties!

I often have people ask me what's it like to be Che and Sue's daughter and to grow up in the Ahn family. I try to respond in as kind a manner possible. I usually say something like, "Being a pastor's kid can be challenging at times but it is extremely rewarding." I rarely elaborate the "challenging" parts, because I don't want to discourage any person from entering the ministry. In fact, I applaud anyone who feels called to the ministry because I have witnessed firsthand the sacrifices my parents continually make. On the other hand, I made an adamant, personal vow (one that I later received inner healing for and broke off) that I would never 1) go into ministry or 2) marry a pastor. It's funny how the things you run away from are the very things you are called to be. And no, I am not married to a pastor but I have certainly devoted my time to ministry.

Ministry and Rejection

My aversion to ministry first began when I was nine years old (1993). It wasn't that I ceased to believe in Jesus or lost respect for the ministry. However, events I could not understand were brewing and would cause me to experience intense, personal collateral damage. I can't recall the specific details surrounding the period when my family was asked to leave the church that they planted and began in 1984. All I remember was the immediate feeling of rejection and confusion. My parents tried to explain to us four children that things would be different, and that God had called our family into a new season of ministry. From the moment my dad stepped down from being the senior pastor of a growing church in Pasadena, I was brutally aware of the discrimination Christians can show to each other. Family friends I knew all my life suddenly severed themselves from any relationship or communication with us. My sense of safety and love within the church was shattered with confusion and doubt, and as a result my faith went into crisis.

It's ironic how the Kingdom of heaven works. You often have to die in order to truly live. God asked my parents to take a life-altering risk and to leave, in love and grace, the church they had planted and the community they had nourished. For me, it was like being wrenched from home and family as it was the only church and community I had ever known. I recently asked my parents about this period of their personal "dark night of the soul." They both responded that although it was hard, it was also the best decision they ever made. They were able to see that what was meant for harm became a "but God" redemptive event. For me, a child at that time, I could not have disagreed with their decision to leave more. I became angry and bitter toward them and blamed them for being the cause of the separation from my extended church family.

My parents did what they knew how to do best and started another church. It first began in our living room and after one month, quickly exploding in size, we had to rent a church building. I remember those beginning days when we were first introduced to a new form of ministry—the prophetic renewal movement. After my dad and ministry partner Lou Engle came back from a trip to Argentina—and later Toronto—ministry as we knew it changed forever. It was different from anything I had ever experienced in that there was no structure to our prayer meetings and worship would last for hours followed by prayer. Often we wouldn't even get to the speaker's message if the Holy Spirit moved strongly. I'm sure our neighbors thought we were crazy or had opened a commune of some sort!

Initially, those prayer meetings were extremely fun for the 10-year-old within me. It turned out that the family friends who separated themselves from us, and whom we weren't allowed to talk to, thought these new meeting times and doing church with the Holy Spirit were pretty amazing too, and they began to secretly attend with us. It's funny how things work out for the good to those who love the Lord! The Lord is so faithful to love us and reveal our purpose and destiny according to His perfect timing.

The Renewal

In 1994, when the outpouring of the Father's love became a revival at the Toronto Airport Fellowship, my dad and Lou Engle went to Canada to seek God for increased revelation and new spiritual impartation. They returned on fire and before I knew it, we were hosting nightly meetings ourselves. During that time, my family virtually lived in Mott Auditorium, the building that held our nightly meetings. The six of us would run over to our little home two miles away to eat, sleep, and then drive back for our nightly meetings.

Those renewal meetings were mind-blowing. We would worship for hours and then have soaking times where we allowed the Holy Spirit to be Lord and lead. At the end of the services, thousands would line up to receive an outpouring of God's love and manifest it through tears of joy, laughter, shouting, jumping, even spinning uncontrollably. Row upon row of people waited for an impartation on that gymnasium floor, hands opened and palms up.

Every day as I stood in that line, I too expected the Holy Spirit to move. Yet every time I received prayer, while everyone else around me was experiencing manifestations of God's presence, I felt as if I was playing a continual game of "last (wo)man standing." I would stand there with my eyes closed more than ever, hands raised a little higher and palms opened a little wider, severely sweating at that point. I was desperate for something, anything from God. I remember that at times I felt so frustrated and embarrassed that I never felt the strong presence of God I would fake being slain in the spirit. I like to call it a "courtesy fall." You know, when you feel so bad for yourself, and even worse for the poor person who's praying for you diligently, hoping the Lord will touch you. It was times like those that I simply became plank-like and fell directly back always peeking behind me to see there was a catcher. If I was going to fake being slain in the spirit then I better be safe doing it! This continued for several years. I would receive prayer and wouldn't feel anything. But I got up, kept believing, and kept asking.

Later in my life, the Lord revealed to me two reasons why I never felt Holy Spirit during those days of renewal. First, I was so consumed with the hype of manifestations that I lost focus on His face and heart. Second, the Lord showed me that He was stretching me to go deeper in my identity in Him. If I could sum up my experience of those renewal days, I would describe myself as a bystander. I was there every day and participated, and yet there was something deeply missing in my heart. I witnessed signs and wonders that I had only known and read about in the Bible or in past revival biographies. My identity was wrapped up with the desperate need to be a part of that movement—to be at every meeting, to experience manifestations of God's presence, to worship with all of my heart—but I was missing the simple yet profound message of my heavenly Father's love. My relationship with Jesus was surface level. I was so fixated on the glitz and glam of the renewal that I bypassed the peaceful, steadfast quietness of the Father's love.

The Beginning of My Depression

In 1997, I eagerly begged my parents to allow me to go to a "regular school" for junior high. Up until that point, all of us were being homeschooled by my mom, a professional teacher who graduated from George Washington University. As the renewal meetings began to slow down, there was such insecurity in my heart in that I wanted to be like my peers. I thought that if I went to a regular school that I would be able to prove my worth and myself. The school my parents enrolled me in was a prestigious private Christian school, and it was during my junior high years that I first fell into deep depression. I remember the first day of school and how awkward and uncomfortable I felt. I didn't know anyone at the school. I was dreading lunch hour when I would pretend I was busy in order to avoid feeling alone for that 30 minutes. Let's just say I spent a lot of my time hanging out in the bathroom stalls, wasting time. However, it really wasn't long before I was able to meet friends, many with whom I still stay in touch with today.

Nevertheless, I gradually grew more and more depressed, and this not only took a toll on my family but my schooling as well. I remember that no matter how hard I tried, I kept falling behind academically. From my junior high to high school years, I separated myself from my family, especially my parents. I was angry, so angry that I refused to have anything to do with them. I was verbally abusive toward my mom and too frightened to be anything other than silent toward my dad. I communicated less and less, seldom showed affection toward my parents, and overall I hated my life.

My resentment toward my parents escalated during high school within my partial lens of my father choosing ministry over family, and equally with my mom for not stopping him. In October 1999, during my freshman year of high school, my father called our whole family together for a meeting. It wasn't abnormal for our family to meet on a consistent basis. In fact, ever since I can remember we've had a once-a-week family day, which typically falls on a Monday. I attribute these family times to the influence of my mother's Filipino culture, where there's always lots of food and noise. With four females in our family, it's an absolute miracle that my brother and dad were able to get a word in edgewise. My dad learned to be heard by just continually talking as if we were actually paying attention. My brother, on the other hand, would employ a different strategy. He would ask the same question over and over again until someone answered him. His approach often failed in frustration and he'd forfeit eventually and quit asking. I never really felt bad for him, because it was, of course, all part of my plan to train my poor, sweet brother for his future wife.

Everything considered, our family times have always been memorable, but this particular family gathering had a different tone. I always knew when we were going to talk about something serious because my dad started the conversation with, "Your mother and I have been praying..." or, "I got a prophetic download." This time was the latter. With all six of us gathered around the small kitchen table, my dad shared how God had asked him to stand with his covenant brother, Lou Engle, and help mobilize for TheCall, Washington DC. TheCall was a massive prayer gathering on the Washington Mall, where 400,000 young people gathered on September 2, 2000 to pray for our nation. All of us, including me, honestly and truthfully released him to obey what God had asked him to do—to serve Lou and to serve TheCall. My relationship with my dad at this point was stagnant. I gladly released my father to mobilize for TheCall, but actually I couldn't have cared less. I didn't understand that the very thing I thought I desired—to be as far away from my dad as possible—was the very thing that would tear me apart within the midst of family-wide crisis. I barely saw my dad for the next three and a half years, the years I was discovering who I was. My depression grew deeper as I wept daily, angry with God, frustrated at my father, and resentful with myself.

The Love of My Parents

My depression escalated and I coped by absorbing myself in school and work. I have always been a person with a strong personality. I used to get comments on my report card that said "often challenges authority" or "disrespectful to leadership." Of course, I never thought I was disrespectful. The way I saw it, I was simply speaking my mind when I thought something was unjust or just plain wrong. During this time, if I wasn't at my friend's house or at school events, I was at work at the local bagel bakery trying to save for my dream car, a red Chevy Blazer SUV. Being the class president and school vice president for three out of my four years in high school mandated that I go to every school event. Naturally, I didn't mind going because it was an excuse to skip certain classes—typically Bible. I figured I grew up being a pastor's kid and had all the Bible lessons I needed. I soon realized that wasn't true when I had to cheat during major tests because I didn't know the material. Later, after I graduated, I confessed to my teacher that I cheated and he forgave me and actually thanked me for repenting. It's funny how life works.

The time I did spend with my parents was limited. I rarely saw my dad, and when I did I wouldn't speak to him. Physical affection between us eroded to the point that I didn't even allow him to touch my shoulder. With my mom, it was a daily battle. I remember her constantly crying because of the harsh words I would say as I purposely wore her down. The thing that I remember most about my mom was the drive home after I was in detention, or after she had to meet with the principal on my behalf. I recall often getting called into the principal's office for too many tardies (my sister and I would stop at Starbucks on the way to school every day) or for being disrespectful toward my teacher. Because I was on student council, the principal made it clear to me that I had to set a good example with my actions, and therefore I had harsher punishments. He called it "Leadership 101," and I called it unfair.

There was never a moment when my mom was angry with me after I had been disciplined by my school. In fact, it was the opposite. There's something about the compassion of a mother that melts the anger of any child. When I deserved further punishment from her, I received love instead. She knew that I was already punished enough with embarrassment and shame. Looking back on my actions I am overwhelmed by the grace and mercy that my mother bestowed on me.

Likewise there were times, during my high school years, when I saw my father's unconditional love. Although I was angry and bitter toward my father, there was something within my heart, like any child, that longed for my father. But with my strong will and pride, I regularly kept him at arm's length. On New Year's Eve 1999 my friends and I were getting ready for the biggest New Year's of our life—2000! Traditionally, our church had a service to enter into the New Year with worship and praise. As a freshman in high school, I made it very clear to my parents that I did not want to be there.

As my parents entered the church service, I devised a plan with two of my friends to ditch the meeting, walk over to the local liquor mart, and pay an adult to buy us a bottle of Smirnoff vodka. I will never forget what the man said to us when we asked him to buy the vodka. "Wow, kids these days are drinking pretty hard stuff." Later I came to full realization of what he meant. Keep in mind, I had no idea what I was doing. This New Year's craze wasn't me. After all, up until this point I had little to no knowledge about alcohol beyond a Bud Light. We rushed back to my house and began to pass the bottle around. When it came to my turn a deep conviction fell upon me, and I suddenly realized what I was doing and refused to take a swig. Looking back, I know it was God because if I had not been sober during what took place next, I would have either been poisoned by alcohol or too incapacitated to seek help for my other friends.

Before long, both my friends had almost consumed the whole bottle of vodka. One instantly began to vomit in the toilet and the other one blacked out. Panic set in for me as I tried to get her to wake up. By this time it was New Year's and I knew that my parents would be coming back any minute from the meeting. The downstairs house door opened and my parents voiced a call out to us. I ran downstairs to seek my parents' help, and they rushed upstairs to aid my friends. As I was crying in fear and regret, my dad took me into my bedroom while my mom cared for my friends in the other room. In the morning my parents told me that my friend had alcohol poisoning, and if she had not vomited, she would have been in severe danger.

Once alone in my room, thoughts began to race through my head. It was because of me that my friend almost died. As I cried on the floor of my bedroom, my dad walked in and sat next to me. He wrapped his arms around me and I allowed myself to fall into his chest. I was at the end of my willpower. I had no pride, no anger, just shame over what I had done. What my dad said next still astounds me. He began to repent and ask me for forgiveness for not protecting us better. He said he felt his lifestyle before he was saved had opened up a door for the enemy to get in. It was at that moment that I felt the intensity of my dad's love for me. Here I was, culpable for what had happened that night, yet he was the one asking me to forgive him! In that moment, my father's unconditional love broke the barriers around my heart. I began to pour out heavy burdens that had been weighing me down for so long. I told him how angry I was with him for choosing ministry over family, how I was so hurt that I never saw him, and how I felt that he simply didn't care about us.

He looked me straight in the eye as I was weeping and said, "Mary do you think I want to leave you? It hurts me every time I leave and have to travel. If I had a choice I would be with you guys all the time, but God asked me to serve your Uncle Lou for TheCall and I need to obey Him." He continued, "Mary, there are people who are suffering and are lost. If they don't hear about the love of Jesus, how else will they be saved? God called me to witness so that His love could set the captives free." For the first time in my 14 years of living, I finally realized the magnitude of my father's calling and ministry. His love for Jesus and conviction to see the suffering set free and saved transcended his natural yearning to stay at home and be with us. In the end, he yielded to Jesus, placing God first and sacrificing his own desires, to see heaven come to earth. At the end of him sharing his heart in vulnerability, he asked me, "Mary, would you like to rededicate your heart to Jesus and live in freedom?" Eyes full of tears I said yes and my father led me through the sinner's prayer for the second time.

I believe New Year's 2000 set a spiritual precedent for the following years of my life. After I rededicated my life to Jesus, I was somewhat more at peace with my father, but there was still something deeply lacking in my heart. I did not understand and live out my true identity as a daughter of our heavenly Father. I quickly fell back into depression that was even worse than before. The rest of high school until late senior year was what you would call "a nightmarish blur."

From Black and White to Color

It was on October 31, 2002, Halloween, when I reached my lowest point. I was in my photography class. My teacher began to read the answers of a homework assignment we turned in to the class members aloud. He stopped at mine and announced to the whole class how ridiculous it was that I got a question wrong. As my teacher continued his criticism, I completely lost it and began to cry hysterically as I sprinted out of the room. I sat outside of school, not caring if I received detention, as I was done. You would've thought that I had walked off a set of the show *Days of Our Lives*. My depression enveloped me and I gave up on life, on my parents, and most importantly God. I went home early from school and slept the rest of the day.

Not wanting to be by myself that night, I joined my parents at our annual revival conference with speakers including James Goll, Jill Austin, and John Arnott. Later the parents of the other authors of this book would be added to our annual conference lineup. There was nothing special about this service. I was completely disengaged as I tried to recover from the day's events. For ministry time my dad announced that we would be having a fire tunnel to ensure that everyone would be able to receive prayer. Because I was so weary of getting prayer and not feeling the presence of God, I had not received ministry in years. But on this particular night when I felt I could go no lower, I made a conscious decision to get in line for the prayer tunnel. In line I remember saying to myself, "Okay God, I give up. I can't do anything more. I have nothing left."

The moment I said that with my heart and soul I walked through the tunnel and was instantly struck with the power of God. Words cannot describe what I felt or experienced. My depression instantly dissipated and I felt freer than ever before. It was as if I had been living my whole life in black and white and suddenly everything was in color. There was such an engulfing love that permeated every fiber of my being. All of my senses were heightened as if I was living in a cave and walked out into the promised land. I could see and sense every spiritual thing around me, and God's voice was as clear as day. The manifestation that I had so longed for as a child came like a rushing wave. It felt like I was going to explode because my body couldn't handle the strong presence of God. For three months after my deliverance I lived in the heavenly realm where my true identity as a daughter of heavenly Father was fully revealed.

The Road to Reconciliation

Since that day, my life has changed. The second greatest miracle after my deliverance from depression was my reconciliation with my parents, beginning with my mom. Kneeling at her feet, I cried into her lap and repented for the years of pain I caused her. As she forgave and embraced me, I felt the Spirit lead me to ask her for a mother's blessing by imparting her spiritual mantle. She prayed over me that I would receive everything and more that the Lord had given her. A shift in my life ensued. I received a higher calling on my life to serve similarly to how He has called my mother to care for women and orphans in developing nations.

Later, in 2003, my dad and I were driving back from church. As we pulled into our driveway, before he got out of the car, I stopped him and told him we needed to talk. God had been speaking clearly to me that I needed to reconcile with my dad, but I was too nervous to do it until that point. I began to repent for my rebellious years, dishonoring him as my father and my spiritual covering. In the same way the Lord led to me ask my mom for a blessing, I asked my father for his blessing and to impart his mantle. We both wept together in the car as he imparted his God-given mantle upon me.

Looking back ten years since receiving my parents' mantles, I still don't know the full extent of what it means. I was simply obeying Holy Spirit. What I do know is that from the time I reconciled with my parents, my relationship with them has dramatically changed. After high school graduation, the Lord instructed me to serve both of my parents where I was, working for my mom in the children's ministry department and my dad as his assistant. It was as if God wanted to take my healing deeper. After I was able to serve and be under my parents' authority and covering, I felt the Lord release me to pursue my own destiny.

Today I am constantly reminded of the Father's amazing love for me. I now live in complete freedom, knowing that He paid the greatest price! I have never fallen back into depression since that Halloween night when heaven came down and the Holy Spirit wrecked my life. As for my relationship with my parents, this one chapter cannot hold the words of love that I have toward them. To date, the reconciliation with my parents is by far the greatest miracle I've experienced in my life. When I thought all was lost, the Lord proved me wrong with His abounding grace and love.

I was recently reminded of how far my relationship with my father has come when I went to see a film adaptation of our family's favorite musical—*Les Misérables*. Sitting next to my dad, I turned to catch a stream of tears falling down his face as Jean Valjean, played by Hugh Jackman, is forgiven by the bishop for stealing the convent silver. As Jean Valjean ended his song devoting his life to be a good and honest man, my dad turned to me and whispered, "This movie is such an example of God's unconditional love by sending His own son to die for our sins." It was true; *Les Misérables* is a picture of Christ and how when we don't deserve to be forgiven and to have second chances, God in His great love and mercy turns around and gives us what we don't deserve—a life of freedom and joy. Jean Valjean's closing remarks still resonate in my heart. He said, "To love another person is to see the face of God." I have been forgiven and redeemed by the unconditional love of my heavenly Father, and therefore I am able to unconditionally love myself, my parents, but most importantly, God.

Although this is my own experience being the daughter of Pastors Che and Sue, I pray that all will find freedom in areas of bondage through the revelation of our great and loving heavenly Father. We, I included, still fall short and struggle in many areas, but the difference between now and ten years ago is that I hold true to the knowledge that I am loved by Jesus no matter what I do or do not do. As Second Corinthians says, "But we all, with unveiled face, beholding as in a mirror the glory of the Lord, are being transformed into the same image from glory to glory, just as from the Lord, the Spirit" (2 Cor. 3:18). As we become more like Him, discovering our true identity within, we too can share in His glory and all He has for our lives.

CHAPTER 7

LIFE AFTER THE ALTER

Joshua Clark

When they reached the place God had told him about,
Abraham built an altar there and arranged the wood on it.
He bound his son Isaac and laid him on the altar,
on top of the wood. Then he reached out his hand
and took the knife to slay his son
(Genesis 22:9-10 NIV, emphasis added).

The story of Abraham's sacrifice is an amazing display of faith and obedience. Confident in God's promises, Abraham believed, if need be, God would raise his son from the dead to fulfill His promise. Thus, Abraham becomes the ultimate example of a man justified by faith— the father of us all (see Rom. 4). Given the celebrity position Abraham holds throughout the Bible, it's easy to read the above passage and forget about the other character—a child, bound and placed on an alter, watching his father hold a knife poised to kill him. Regardless of Abraham's faith in the matter, it is unclear whether Isaac believed similarly. And while much ink has been spilled detailing the "sacrifice of Abraham," next to nothing has been spent seeing the world through Isaac's eyes.

What follows is my personal story, along with what the Holy Spirit is teaching me—daily—about the importance of reconciliation and relationship. In sum: how to live life *after* the altar.

On Being

Random, well-intentioned conference attendee: "So, what is it like living with your dad?"

This question, and its infinite permutations, has dominated my life. Like clockwork, within seconds of discovering my identity as Randy Clark's son, people would ask about my experiences. I get it— inquiring minds want to know. Undoubtedly. You are, in fact, reading this book.

Still, as a young boy, I couldn't help but wonder—*why?* Or, more aptly, *To what end?* To those merely curious (this was before reality TV sated our voyeuristic desires), I wondered, *Why not go buy one of the many books off the table in the back?* It felt like much of our lives was detailed in my father's books and newsletters. Stop being lazy, or worse, cheap. To those looking for comfort, solace, or any other equally significant experience, I failed to see how my story could help. I viewed my experiences as mine. Whatever stuff I dealt with or privileges I received, that journey was mine. The circumstances of my youth were proprietary, or so I thought, and my victories and failures ill-suited for alternative application. I didn't think my life was special or "better than." Merely mine. My cross to bear, my road to travel. Accordingly, my standard response to the above interrogatory was a nondescript, "It's normal." Only rarely, when I sensed growing dissatisfaction with that answer, would I cheekily add, "Just kidding. It's everything you're imagining and more. So much more."

Don't worry. I've long since repented for these youthful transgressions. Additionally, I've come to realize the value of my story.

In Second Corinthians 5:18, the apostle Paul writes that the reconciled have become reconcilers. My personal belief is that the experiences, struggles, defeats, and victories one has along the road of life inform the reconciliation process. They fill the process full with meaning by answering the question, "What have we been reconciled *from?*" We are particularly well-suited to reconcile those who are similarly situated. One's pre-reconciliation weaknesses become his greatest post-reconciliation weapons against the powers of darkness. I recognize that I have been reconciled from a life—similar to many, both secular and Christian—replete with issues of doubt, abandonment, and disillusionment. It is for those that struggle with these afflictions that I write, in hopes of planting (or watering) seeds of reconciliation. To that end, the stories contained herein are the complete (to the best of my ability) retelling of the formative events of my life. In full disclosure, this is not intended as a biography and many wonderful tales have been omitted; those experiences, memories, and stories not relevant to the topic of reconciliation will remain mine, until the Holy Spirit requires them in writing.

I was born in southern Illinois to a loving mother and a playful (and equally loving) father. Regrettably, time has wizened my memories of this era, but a few precious remnants remain. Regular trips in my Radio Flyer wagon along undulating—and to a five year old, never-ending— cobblestone roads; an entire room filled with electric trains and tracks; little green Army men platoons, complete with Lincoln Log bunkers, sprawled along the family room floor. In all these memories, there is one constant—my dad. He pulled my wagon without tires, constructed train track configurations without fail, and set up hundreds of Army men, only to have me knock them over with Lincoln Log grenades seconds later and ask for him to "do it again" without complaint. In truth, I have few early memories that don't include my dad playing with me in some form or fashion.

When I was five, my parents felt called to plant a church in St. Louis, Missouri. At first this meant weekly road trips to Missouri, with me frantically scanning the horizon to be the first to spot the Arnold, Missouri water tower—a sign we were close to our destination and yet another game my dad and I would play. Soon it became clear that St. Louis would become our new home, and near the end of '86 my family moved.

We lived for the first seven or so months in a hotel. I blame this season, and the moral hazard it provided, for my inability to clean up after myself. After the hotel, we moved into the lone condominium complex of an aborted project (funding had apparently dried up before the additional units were constructed). The complex was predominated with the elderly. Predictably, I made no real friends here, but was dutifully doted on by the elderly. For my part, I gladly filled the gap left by grandchildren who no longer had time to visit and learned an invaluable lesson—old people have candy everywhere! When I wasn't sucking down butterscotch lozenges, I spent my time swimming and running errands. By nine, I was doing most of the family grocery shopping—alone. My mom would scrawl out a list onto the back of an envelope and then give me a signed blank check, which I would walk up the hill, through the condominium parking lot, and across the street to the nearest grocery store. Though shocked at first, the cashiers quickly warmed up to the nine-year-old shopper, and it wasn't long till I was on first-name basis with the day shift.

My parents, busy with church planting, were gone most nights, leaving me to watch my sister—and eventually also my brother. People laugh in disbelief when I tell them at nine I would regularly (read: four or five nights a week) watch my four-year-old sister. But it was normal to us. Only once did things go poorly. During a failed reenactment of the final scene of *Karate Kid*, my crane kick—truly unblockable—knocked my little sister into the brick fireplace mantle, leaving a large gash in her head and blood on the floor. After that, we stopped mimicking *Karate Kid* maneuvers—replaced it with *The Princess Bride*. My sister is an excellent fencer now. Normally my parents would return home around 10:00 P.M. and we'd all curl up together to watch *The Love Connection, Leave it to Beaver,* and *I Love Lucy.* Due to my parents' grueling schedule, I was allowed to miss (or, at least, I did miss) every Monday from elementary school. On these brief reprieves, we'd fish, play at a park, and lounge at the pool. All in all, I greatly enjoyed my childhood.

Concerning my spiritual development, my parents took a "pincer attack" approach. My mother would only let me listen to Christian worship music (and it played nonstop, all day long, literally). My dad would only read me Christian books (usually biographies of famous missionaries or evangelists, but occasionally something more age appropriate like *The Chronicles of Narnia*). Again, my memories have mostly faded but I do have a vague recollection of my dad reading to me quite frequently, though I'm not sure when he found the time. Life continued on in much the same way for the next five to ten years until, in 1994, my dad (and I) would take a trip to Toronto that would change the fate of our family forever.

Originally scheduled for only a few nights, the Toronto meetings spanned months and kept my dad busy long after I had returned home. Revival had broken out, and with the Toronto Blessing in full swing, I spoke with my dad—over the phone—only a few times throughout the next six weeks. His absence was felt most acutely by my mother, who had only been away from him for a couple days throughout their entire 20-plus year marriage. Though my siblings and I had become accustomed to my parents working hard and being gone most nights, we saw them quite frequently during the day. With my dad now away in Toronto, not only did we lose our morning and afternoon play partner, but my mother experienced the pressure and responsibility of solely tending to four children. This, coupled with her own loss, made for a difficult time. Still, we lumbered on together, naively thinking this revival was but a discrete episode, an isolated occurrence that wouldn't change the status quo. We were wrong.

Quickly it became clear that things would never be the same. When not in Toronto, Dad was fielding calls and requests to visit other churches and speak at even more conferences. Unsure how long he would be sought after, my dad took every engagement offered. Seemingly overnight he went from being home (in some form or fashion) every night to traveling 220-plus days a year.

My brothers (two and four at the time) grew up in this feverish period, and as such, think of it as normal. My sister and I (eight and thirteen)—shocked by the sudden change—felt the loss more, particularly me, who, as a soon-to-be-adolescent, needed his dad. Our family got into a routine after a while—Mom would manage the household (as best she could) while Dad was away for weeks at a time; Dad would take us to Chuck-E-Cheese, Discovery Zone, and movies on his return. Rinse and repeat.

After a few months, we settled into a rhythm and tried to make do. When it became obvious this "new normal" was going to be around for the foreseeable future, I began to travel with my dad, especially during the summer months. I got to see much of the world during this time and was exposed to many amazing teachings, signs, and wonders. Regrettably, these few episodic trips couldn't fill the void growing in my heart for a deeper relationship with my dad. As that void approached critical mass, I filled it with substitutes, as hurting people often do. With the inadequacy of these substitutes apparent, I put God there. Or, I tried. It wasn't really God, more of a placeholder for where a real relationship with God would go, if I had one.

Somewhere along the way, I attributed the absence of my natural father to my spiritual one. Though I was mad at neither, I stopped trying to communicate with either. And like muscles never used, my ability to relate atrophied. When I talk to others who have experienced perceived abandonment (because I was never *really* abandoned), they are angry, bitter. Most of my friends who had doctors or lawyers for parents were mad at their absence or at the emotional toll on the family caused by the constant working. Many continue to be angry, refusing to have any relationship with their parents. To me, though—one who had witnessed the amazing, life-changing things my dad was doing—it felt unbelievably selfish to be mad. I believed the great harvest of souls my dad was reaping was more important than my present suffering. I remembered my dad's stories of the great missionaries, like Adoniram Judson, who buried many wives and children in the soil of Burma for the gospel. My dad was—literally—changing people's lives. How could I be angry at his absence, induced by spiritual obedience, or at a gracious God who was powerfully at work rescuing, redeeming, and restoring His people? Instead, I did what humans are so well designed to do—adapt. I became accustomed to his absence and eventually my dad became a stranger to me. An amazingly magnanimous and gracious stranger, but a stranger nonetheless.

In retrospect, I think anger is a healthier alternative. Anger signals a present vested interest in a relationship. An angry person's emotions recoil at the thought of separation and passionately want things to be different. And, while I would *wish* for things to be different, I had accepted that they couldn't and moved on with my life. My path portended the end of an interest. Absence may make the heart grow fonder, but extended absence can make it grow cold and distant. My body, mind, and emotions eventually rewired themselves to make me think I didn't need this type of interaction. After a decade of travel, I felt I didn't *need* to have a relationship with my dad, couldn't have one if I wanted. Only many years later, encouraged by the Holy Spirit to make intentional choices toward restoration, would my desire for relationship be reignited.

To be fair, my dad's traveling is not entirely to blame for my awkwardness. When I was very young my parents received a prophetic word that led them to believe I would end up in ministry. My dad was never shy to shout this presumably foregone conclusion from the rooftop. It felt like every conversation I had with my parents was about this eventuality. It was like my dad was the Mayor of Whoville and I was JoJo. Of course this isn't an accurate depiction, but the hormones of adolescence are powerful psychogenic drugs and it felt like every discussion was about my eventual succession to the throne of international ministry, which I had no desire to ascend. The awkwardness created by my dad's absence, my perception of his goals for me, and my inability—or lack of desire—to meet those expectations led to my distancing myself from my family. I moved out at seventeen, went away to college, and—like the prodigal son before me—had no plans to return. Ever.

But.

Thankfully.

God is good. All the time. He sought me out, like the shepherd who left the ninety-nine. He ran *to* me, He revealed His sufficiency, His grace, His mercy, and displayed His commitment to my well-being. He prompted me to meditate on the story of Abraham and Isaac, the awkwardness of the walk back down the mountain after such a traumatic event, the resulting dysfunction in the family (arguably rooted in Isaac's experience), and despite all of it, His purposes and promises, which are always good, were accomplished. Jesus still came, made a way for us to enter boldly before the King, and blessed us with the Holy Spirit.

I eventually moved back to the same city as my parents and began serving their ministry in a variety of administrative and support functions. Throughout the next decade, God taught me a lot about reconciliation. He blessed me with a wife, three beautiful children, and restored to me an amazing family (once lost and hidden by my pain) with whom to walk this journey out. So, in looking back over the last decade, what can I share that might help expedite your journey?

On Overcoming

1. Get Perspective

It's easy to feel detached and isolated in the midst of a spiritual and emotional storm. The first step toward freedom is to recognize our tendency to become self-absorbed. Ask the Holy Spirit to realign your focus to see your troubles through His eyes. For me, the Lord reminded me of a saying my dad was fond of saying: "Don't throw the baby out with the bathwater." I found it instructive because I was clearly disregarding many of the wonderful lessons I had learned through my time with my dad. By asking the Holy Spirit to reveal the good times, calluses began to fall off my heart. I saw clearly the things I had forgotten, the things blinded by pain and indifference. I realized how profoundly grateful and honored I should be. My dad, despite his absence, had modeled a lifestyle of many amazing attributes. In fact, parents would be hard-pressed to find better models to pattern themselves after. A couple big ones that made a tremendous impact include authenticity, openness, generosity, and humility.

I always felt like I had my dad's ear, as if anything I would say would be considered seriously. No matter the importance of the conference call or the meeting, my parents welcomed me to the table to listen and share my opinions. Even before I became a teenager and knew everything. I credit this for my confidence in the Lord and steadfast faith in His ability to accomplish His desires. I've always believed that if I were to ask God for something—anything—He would answer. My parents' open door policy cultivated in me a quiet confidence that assured me of my value, position, and importance.

Another benefit (at least I view it as one) of my parents' openness and transparency was that I saw firsthand the sometimes seedy underbelly of church life and ministry. At first it was deflating, like when a child first realizes his dad *isn't* Superman. People I had known my whole life through church or ministry were secretly hurting, struggling with their own past wounds and demons. And this wasn't just recent converts or newly elected elders, but "big names" in the charismatic movement who had huge megachurches and large, successful ministries. After many years of exposure to this reality, I became even more amazed at God's grace and faithfulness. While other pastor's kids around me grew cynical with their exposure to this, I couldn't help but fall even more in love with the grace of God. To be sure, it's tragic when a believer stumbles, or when a secret lifestyle is exposed, but I tend to believe we—the church—make it a much bigger deal than God, the Father.

Lest I be misinterpreted, the above should not be construed as an attempt to sweep sin under the rug or mitigate its devastating effects. This is only a realization that 1) God is God—He uses the tools available to Him, even when those tools have rust, scrapes, and dents that might appear to disqualify them for service; and 2) God is the God of second chances, and third chances, and fourth chances, and fifth…well, you get the idea. Sanctification, for me, is a spectrum along which many, even those in ministry, are left of center. To be sure, this is nothing to celebrate, and we should all strive to live a holier life, holding our leaders to biblical standards. None of these truths, however, prevent me from boasting in the Lord's goodness and graciousness for using broken vessels.

Another aspect of my upbringing that the Holy Spirit illuminated was my dad's humility. As a teenager, I didn't realize the rarity of this trait. I naively assumed most would recognize their weakness apart from God. Surprisingly, many do not. My dad's insistence on activating everyone for the work of the ministry, hoping to "equip his way out of a job" still ministers to my spirit. Recent research indicates that those who gain power via fame, a promotion, or the like become less hospitable and friendly to those underneath them. My dad eschewed any attempt to elevate his name. He was much happier, and more comfortable, with seeing Jesus' name held in high esteem. By regarding himself a lowly servant, he remained compassionate and empathetic to the many people he ministered to nightly. But I digress. I could go on for chapters (and someday maybe I will) but I'm skirting dangerously close to going "off topic."

The above was what the Holy Spirit used to provide perspective to my problem. Seek out what He would say to yours. There is always something good and redeemable to be found in the midst of even immense pain; *don't throw the baby out with the bathwater.* Ask the Holy Spirit to illuminate these areas in your life.

2. Choose Wisely

Along with being the iconic phrase from the end of *Indiana Jones and the Last Crusade*, the above is a reminder that we are not slaves to our past hurts, fears, or emotions. God is big on choice. He hopes we choose Him, but allows us the ability to not. We have within us the power to align ourselves with the blueprint of heaven or disregard His dreams and aspirations for our lives and live how we please. He is unashamed of providing us with this opportunity; He placed the tree of the knowledge of good and evil in the *center* of the garden, and made it bloom with beautiful fruit! As best I can tell, there was no barbed wire fence, or moat, or animal feces strewn about the tree to dissuade Adam or Eve, only His lone admonishment. Though the Lord knew the unbelievable turmoil He and the earth would experience, He freely—with open hands—allowed His creations to find their way in the world.

Choice is a big deal. And in life, we always have a choice. A choice to be negative, cynical, or depressed. A choice to continue ruminating on all the bad things that have happened. Or a choice to be joyous, even in the midst of our sorrow. Darkness begets more darkness, but even the smallest point of light can begin to light a path to freedom. Diligently train your mind, will, and emotions to be full of joy, eagerly anticipate the full manifestation of God's glory. Be of good cheer! Jesus has overcome the world and in doing so has made a way for your total healing and restoration.

Don't mistake my encouragement to choose joy as a suggestion to sweep your pain under the rug and put on a good Christian front. Hardly. Fully embrace your pain, talk about it, scream about it, cry about it, whatever the Holy Spirit leads you to do, do it. Remember that Jesus was asleep, in peace, on a boat that was being buffeted in a storm because the reality He lived in had no storms. With help, pass through your pain and step into this reality. Henri Nouwen said it best when he wrote, on the topic of overcoming pain, "You have to begin to trust that your experience of emptiness is not the final experience, that beyond it is a place where you are being held in love."

3. Step Out of the Boat

I know people who have had relationships supernaturally restored by the power of the Holy Spirit. Decades of hurt, neglect, and trauma were wiped away in an instant, forever forgotten by both parties. I pray this happens with you. For others, however, the road is a bit longer. I mentioned earlier that my relationship muscles atrophied from many years of disuse. After creating in me a spirit of gratitude toward my family by giving me His perspective, and after I had been encouraged by the Holy Spirit to choose life, joy, and relationship, the only thing left was to implement His plan. That proved the most scary, most difficult. I wasn't sure how, or when, or where. It was clear though that I had to act before God was going to move. So, slowly, in fits and starts I began initiating contact with my dad, breaking off years of rust in the process. I felt my heart warm and expand in the process. The awkwardness gave way to familiarity. I was intentional about cultivating a relationship and building a stronger bond with my family. My wife and I recently turned down many lucrative job offers that would take us far away from our families because we felt the Lord was calling us create generational inheritances for our kids. I only saw my grandparents once a year, and I think there is something powerful about children growing up exposed regularly to their ancestors. Again, this is what the Holy Spirit has directed my family to do. Your mileage may vary and no judgment for those who elect to live differently. But whatever you do, take risks, press for the limits of your faith. I had always thought I would move to a big city and make lots of money. I had the opportunity to do both. Ultimately God beckoned me to come stand on the water with Him and trust that He would provide.

4. Beware the Pendulum

Having graduated from school long ago, I (thankfully) no longer make use of Newton's third law. Still, the principle behind the law is important—every action has an equal and opposite reaction. For every hurting person I encounter, I can see this law at work. Those who experienced abusive leadership in church seek organic house church movements where leadership is completely decentralized; those whose childhood lacked structure, wealth, love, whatever, seek to remedy that problem in their own life. This isn't wrong. God knows no one has found the perfect theology, the perfect parenting style, the perfect system of government. I advise you, however, before implementing any changes—or making vows never to do this thing, or that thing—to seek the Lord.

In many ways this comes back to the baby and the bathwater. Not everything from your negative experiences should be discarded. Recognize man's tendency to over-correct and move from one extreme to the next, like a pendulum swinging back and forth. Eventually the pendulum will come to rest in the center, at a place of balance, but how many generations will pass before that happens? Ask the Holy Spirit to open your eyes to your biases and give you fresh insight into the models of government, parenting, church planting, etc. that will help you grow in the fullness of Christ.

The Bible is full of tension. I could write a book on the tension between ministry and family, among other things. Just quickly—recognize the tension in the gospel between loving your wife (family) as Christ loved the church and being willing to sacrifice everything for His Kingdom. I'm not sure the early missionaries, evangelists, or even my parents got it right, and maybe the revelation of Christ in the Bible should inform our understandings of Old Testament passages, or even Paul's personal beliefs, but be careful to not revolt against perceived injustice to the point of idolatry of family or extermination of pastoral leadership. I believe there is room for a paradigm shift in our understanding of community, relationship, and family, so by all means, think outside the box. But in all things, seek the Holy Spirit, lest your hurts lead you to inhabit a deserted island and wrap tinfoil on your head.

On Endings

I don't know how my story will end, or where God will ultimately lead us. Perhaps, to my parent's everlasting joy, I'll end up—officially—in ministry. Still, like the amazing parents they are, they are completely supporting and blessing my choice to enter the legal profession. Regardless of *what* I'm doing, I know that I will be forever grateful to a God who softened my heart to the point of melting and restored everything the enemy tried to tear asunder. I so love and appreciate my dad and mom. Through their life of constant sacrifice and obedience,

I witnessed gospel living as normal, everyday life. The enemy tried to blind me to the amazing value of my experiences and the blessings I received via my parents. Thankfully, God called me out of darkness, killed the fatted calf, and covered me with a robe of righteousness. I know He is ready, willing, and able to do that same for all those that call on His name. For those reading this who struggle with relating with God, earthly parents, siblings, whomever, I pray that the Holy Spirit would begin to work miracles in your life.

CHAPTER 8

A JOURNEY OF LOVE

By Joshua Frost

"Joshua, would you please come into the living room? I need to speak with you." *Uh oh,* was my first reaction. You know what I mean, that first sense of, *What have I done now?* I was playing GI Joes in my bedroom and really resented being interrupted during my playtime. At that moment, nothing was more important to me then seeing my Joes destroying the works of Cobra and his evil forces. But I listened, with an attitude, and started walking toward the living room. While walking I heard the crying of my sister and wondered, *Oh no, what is going on?* I entered the living room to see my father kneeling over a bowl of water that had my sister's feet in it. He was washing her feet and asking her to forgive him of all the wrongs that he had ever done to her. Now it was my turn, and he called me over to the seat. I sat down and he placed my feet into the bowl. Thinking to myself all the while, *This is gross, my sister's feet were just in here.* He started to pray over me while washing my feet. Then he pulled out a sheet of paper and started listing off things that he had done to me in the past that had hurt me. While reading the list he started crying, which in turn made me cry.

He looked into my eyes and said, "Joshua, do you forgive me for all the times that I misrepresented the Father's love to you?"

Of course, in tears I jumped out of my seat, threw my arms around his neck, and said, "Yes, Daddy, I forgive you."

Every child wants to hear the words, "I love you, son." Words that are not spoken to motivate a performance from the child but are words that affirm the child's right to believe they belong. These were the parents I grew up with. My dad was not always this kind and soft-hearted. My siblings knew a different father. One that was emotionally detached, who had no clue how to love his own family. Being the youngest of three children, I did not experience much of my father's dysfunctional behavior before he had this transformation in the Father's love. I had only heard the stories of Captain Bligh and the terror he would inflict in the hearts of everyone he met.

By the age of 21 my father was known as one of the best fishing boat captains on the east coast of the southern US. His drive in life was to become top hook (the best fisherman with the biggest load of fish every time he came to the dock). It did not matter who got hurt along the way to achieving that goal. He had learned that if you are to be noticed in life you must outdo everyone around you.

His entire life he performed for the love of others. Growing up under the roof of a great tennis coach and World War II veteran, my father was trained to be the best at everything he did. His father would not show him any type of love unless he proved that he was the best at what he was doing. Never did my father hear the words *I love you* until he was 20 years old. In the hospital in a drug-induced coma not expected to live, he heard his dad finally say, "Jack, I love you!" Living in the shadow of his older brother's stardom in college tennis, my father did not feel that he had a right to be in his father's presence unless he out-performed everyone around.

His father, Barney, grew up with no father, no one to help him develop in life. Known as the town bastard, other kids were not allowed to play with this fatherless boy. Barney grew up as an orphan and determined that he would raise his sons better than he was raised. His greatest mistake in trying to do something right was he tried to live his life-long dreams through his sons. Driving them to succeed instead of guiding them to destiny fulfilled. This developed a habit structure with the Frost men that you have to beat everyone else at everything you do in order to have value. My father, in turn, judged his dad for not fathering with love and acceptance, causing the cycle to continue.

This learned behavior followed my dad, Jack, even after he was saved and in Bible school. He had to have the best grades, lead the most people to the Lord, pray the most, and read the Bible the most. If my dad did not finish his daily list of survival at being the best, he was often left with the sense of feeling as if he had no value in life. If you cannot beat everyone else at what they do, then you do not have a right to *be*.

Growing up, life for my father was all about "the look." "The look" he would see in his father's face if he did or did not perform right. If he was "top hook," the captain of the boat bringing in the most fish, he got the look of praise, love, and joy. But if he was not the best then he got the look of disappointment or anger. "The look" that sends the silent message, *You don't measure up in my eyes or heart.* But the other look is what we are all looking for. You know that look—the look that should send the message of unconditional love and acceptance. When performance is demanded, acceptance is withheld until you accomplish your task.

Most of my father's life he did not find that place of acceptance and love in his father's eyes. This led him to become just like his father. There are laws of relationship in operation in everyone's life. The law of "when you judge someone you become like the one you judge" began to have consequences now in my own dad's life. Many years later my father found himself with a family of his own. A Christian now, but his identity was still rooted in the character of Captain Bligh. He treated his family the same way his father had treated him years ago. My father never physically abused us like his father did to him, but he did make us earn and perform for his love like his father made him. *You see, how you believe you have to earn love or acceptance from God and others is how you will make others gain your love and acceptance.* One of the major weaknesses of my father was his need for excellence through your performance. It was hard for him to rest or show love and acceptance without your first giving him something or doing something for him.

One day, as I was pouring myself a drink of water in the kitchen I accidently dropped my cup and water went everywhere. My father jumped out of his chair, rushed over, gave me the "look of disappointment," and said, "You better clean that up." It was cases like this that made my early childhood always feel like I had to walk on eggshells around my dad. Anytime I would mess up around him I was always scared he would go off on me or just give me that look of disgust. This left me always feeling like I needed to perform for his

love. Which was the very thing my fath
and judged his earthly father for.

Then one day my father came hom
had attended. There was a man there by the nan
asked my dad if he had ever been blessed by his σa
prayed a father's blessing, and it forever changed how my υ
his own family. God does have a sense of humor. In case you did ι
catch that, Jack Winter prayed for Jack Frost to receive a revelation of
the Father's love.

When I next saw my dad after this encounter, I could just feel
there was something different about him. He explained to us children
what had happened to him at these meetings and how he had had
this amazing encounter with God's love. Still being young, I did not
really fully understand what he was saying. I was kind of off in my
own world thinking about how I could beat the next video games or
surf the next wave. Then, over time, I saw how different he treated his
children and my mom, his wife. I saw how much softer he was toward
us all. I wondered, though, how long this was going to last. It lasted.
He exchanged the old Captain Bligh behavior for a father who really
wanted to know how to love and affirm his family.

During my middle school years, I began to have difficulty with
academics in school. To cover up my struggle with this I began to find
ways to amuse my other classmates, thus taking the focus off of my
issue. One day my teacher called my dad, desperate for an answer on
how to handle me. How my father chose to handle this has impacted
my life forever. At that time I was in eighth grade, and just like any
other middle schooler I wanted to be the life of the party. There was

...em with this, I did not think, except I tended to try to be ...e of the party during class while my teachers were trying to ...n. That did not really go over well with my teachers. Letters were ...t home, consequences were given to me to try and motivate me to change my behavior, but none of it seemed to have any effect on me at all. I continued to misbehave in class by disrupting the flow of the teachers. Frustrated with my behavior, my teachers met and decided that my homeroom teacher should contact my parents for more help with why I continued to get worse in school. They said that I was a bright student, got good grades, but just always wanted to be the life of the party or the class clown. One teacher even admitted that what made it so hard was, "He is really naturally funny, and it becomes hard for me not to laugh, so I do not lose control over the class." My dad told the teachers that he would take care of it and thanked them for calling him.

I came home from school that day feeling particularly good about my day and how life went. As soon as I walked through the door, my father called me into his office. He asked me how my day was. Thinking back on a couple of good comments I had made in class that day, I responded with great confidence that I had had a really great day. I remember telling Dad how much fun I had that particular day. He responded, "How did your teachers like the way you were behaving today?"

"Well they just do not get a joke," I responded.

After grounding me for a week, he said, "If it happens again you are going to get a spanking." But being 13 years old, my father had told me I was too old for spankings so this did not seem like much of a deterrent for me. I told myself, *He is just saying that. He will never really spank me again; I am too old.*

After a couple of weeks of great behavior I started getting bored in class. So once again I went to my old ways of making class less boring and more fun, and once again all three of my teachers called home on the same day. The way my father tells the story is that he was glad I was not home when they called because he would have killed me. Very frustrated with how to handle me, my dad did what he should have done a long time prior to my teachers calling home. He went into his office and asked Father God how he should handle this situation without misrepresenting the Father's love to me.

When I got home from school, my father called me into his office. I knew that this was it—my life as I had known it was about to come to an end, because my expectation was my father was about to go off on me. I walked into the room and he said, "Joshua, I do not know what else to do to help you solve this problem. It is time for a spanking. It's going to be five hits with Mr. Smack." As a child I had been quite familiar with Mr. Smack. Mr. Smack on one side had a colorful set of lips and the other side was his name written in big bold letters and a saying: "Have a kiss from Mr. Smack." He was the five-gallon paint stirrer my parents used to discipline us when everything else failed. So to be confronted with Mr. Smack as a teenager let me know I had gone too far with my behavior.

But to my surprise, instead of me bending over the couch, my father bent over the couch and took the position for me to smack him. He said, "Okay Josh, hit me five times as hard as you can."

I said, "Why?"

He responded, "Because I have evidently failed you as a father. I know of nothing else that will change you. So I need to be disciplined for my bad fathering skills. So I want you to hit me five times as hard as you can. Come on, Joshua, smack me now."

I started crying and said, "No, Dad, I cannot punish you for what I did wrong. I am sorry, Daddy, I will stop misbehaving the first time the teachers ask me to stop." Notice I promised my dad the first time I was asked to stop, I would. You see, I knew I am not a perfect kid. I needed to allow time for my behavior that had become a habit to begin a process of change in my life.

This revealed to me how much of a changed father I really had. Before his encounter with love I would have been the one getting the punishment. But after my father's encounter with love it was this new father who stood in for me to receive punishment for my sins against his love and fathering me. It was my rebellion, my sin, yet he was willing to stand in and take punishment on my behalf. This is the true heart of love, that you would lay down your life for another.

This is the love that God showed the world by giving us His only Son to die for our sins. He took on our punishments so that we would not have to. This is the story of love that is revealed throughout the Bible. The story of a loving Father who loves His people with all of His heart, and a people who love their God back with all of their heart. This situation taught me the grace of God, but it wasn't till years later that I would finally find God's love for myself.

Growing up in this amazing Christian home, it was hard at times for me to personally feel God. I lived most of my life knowing I was a Christian but never experiencing His love for myself. I always lived my Christianity through my parents and it was never real for me. A hardship of growing up in a Christian environment all my life was losing the sense of the awe of God. This is something that you must discover for yourself. I had to go on this journey of seeking love that started for me a year before my birth. You see, I was a promise of God to my parents.

In 1985 my parents were the Salvation Army officers in Horry and Georgetown counties in South Carolina. Newly commissioned to this area, my mom, a very lively character, who was used to having a lot of friends around her for support, found herself in a life situation with so many dysfunctional people who seemed to want to suck the life right out of her. She was very used to hectic schedules, having received her own degree of 189 hours in two years with the Salvation Army Bible College. This, by the way, is almost equivalent to a master's degree in two years, so you can image how busy my parents had been. Both graduating with honors while caring for my other two siblings left them with very little energy to love.

It did not take very long for my parents to begin to feel overwhelmed with their daily duties of running a two-county operation and trying to love their family. My mom finally had all she could handle and basically had a minor breakdown. My father had just recently met some spirit-filled Christian men who seemed really full of joy no matter how their lives were going. It was one of these men, Lynnwood Wilson, who was able to help my mom to overcome the seemingly overwhelming daily life chores so she could find joy again. On the day my mom had her breakdown, instead of taking her to the hospital my dad decided to find Lynnwood and have him pray for them. While driving down a two-lane highway from Conway, South Carolina to Georgetown, my parents had a very supernatural visitation from God.

My parents lived their lives in a constant state of overwhelming stress, to the point that my mom began to cry uncontrollably. All of a sudden my dad began to speak in a voice my mom had never heard. His eyes were closed, yet he was the driver of the vehicle. Not having experienced a heavenly encounter before, this scared my mom. The voice told her that she would next year at this time have a son, to name him Joshua Andrew Frost, and that his purpose in life was to be a warrior for souls in the Kingdom. A warring evangelist for the Kingdom of Heaven of some type. Being already on overload, my mom was dazed by all that had just happened, but like Mary it was so supernatural that her spirit was willing to accept this as from the Lord.

My parents had two older children at this point in their lives. My brother is eight years older than me and my sister is five years older, so my mom actually thought she was done with having any more children. She had had difficulty bearing children and depression afterward so this was not the best news my mom could have received, especially now. But a year later I was born because my parents accepted me as a supernatural gift to them from God.

Growing up I always knew what I was called to do. Mom and Dad constantly told me the story surrounding my birth. I was to be a warring evangelist for Jesus. But I never experienced Jesus for myself. I never had that encounter that I saw my father have. I too wanted an encounter with love but did not know how to get it. After pondering this most of my lifetime, I gave up and started pursuing the things my friends were into.

At the age of four is when my father first pushed me into my first wave surfing. Since that day I was hooked on surfing. Growing up as a surfer is a wonderful thing, but getting caught up in the culture cannot be good at times. Seeking an encounter with God and not finding it made me turn to this culture of surfing for value and purpose. The culture of surfing is made up of people who are trying to escape from the reality of finding and living their destinies. It is actually built on the stronghold of rebellion in the lives of many surfers. This culture has, for the most part, become so overwhelmed with trying to figure life out that they turn to drugs and partying as another means of escape from the realities of responsibility. Their mindset is "screw the world, let's surf."

Now not all surfers are like this but the ones I had gotten involved with were. Your desire, as a surfer in this culture, is to get high, hang out with friends, and surf the next good swell. By the time I reached the age of thirteen I started doing drugs. This is what my life was about for the next four years. I did not care who I hurt and who got in my way. I just wanted to have fun and fulfill my own desires in surfing. This behavior developed a habit of independence that later turned into rebellion. I wanted to do everything my way or it was not going to get done at all. During this time period, if you wanted to give me advice you could screw off and if you got in my way surfing I would yell at you and tell you to go home.

My life was all about me and my crew of friends I hung out with called the "Sweetflow Mafia." Because I built this wall of independence in my life, I could not find God's love. There were times throughout my youth that I tried to seek after God but could never find His love, that love that I so desired and knew was so real. The more I sought Him and could not find Him the more independent I became. After graduating high school I found a job in a local surf shop. While working at Island Inspired I learned how to shape surfboards. My goal in life at this point was to figure out a way to be a part of the surfing industry. Whether it was through surfing films or making surfboards, I did not care.

After working there for a couple months my father started to notice that I was going down a bad path. I was rebelling against my calling to be a warrior evangelist. Instead of becoming a warrior I was becoming a rebel. Living my life opposite and opposed to my destiny. I remember my parents would always try to talk to me about where my life was going. They would tell me that I was acting like a rebel but was called to be a warrior. I am a huge *Star Wars* fan, and every time my parents would tell me I was being a rebel, I would respond with, "The rebels in *Star Wars* were the good guys. Look at Yoda and Luke Skywalker." Over and over they tried to remind me of my destiny and tried to help me see what I was called to do, but my heart was still too hard to find this love I so desired.

Ed Piorek has a saying that actually helped to reshape my life: "When you are strong you cannot find God's love, but it is when you are weak God's love finds you." Because of my walls of independence I was too strong to find His love, but it took an encounter with God to finally soften my heart. My father told me about a school in Maui Hawaii called "Youth with a Mission." He explained to me what the school was about and how they teach people what Christianity is all about. What sold me on this particular school was that my parents would pay for everything and I would be able to surf almost every day. Of course I jumped at the opportunity to be able to surf Hawaii for free.

Hawaii is known for its amazing surf. It had always been a dream of mine to surf the "Big Waves" around the world. My desire to go to the school was never to find God but only to find surf. But God tricked me without my realizing it. His plan for my life would unfold, and that desire to find only the next great wave would change.

A couple of weeks before leaving for Maui I was surfing in a local surf contest and fell off my board and got stabbed in the eye by my surfboard fin. What happened was I was hanging five and I went to hang ten and just nose-dived into the water. After falling, I looked up to see where my board was and the fin of my board hit me right in the eye. I instantly went into shock thinking my eye was hanging out of my head because I was bleeding everywhere. I could not see out of that eye which led me to believe something major was wrong. My friend paddled up to me in the water and asked what I was doing. I turned around and he yelled, "Oh my God!" Which did not help matters. He got me onto the beach and found someone to drive me to the ER. After a couple of eye tests, it was evident I did not have any major damage to the eyeball. I only had a cut on my face and a cut on the white part of my eye. Apparently the eye heals itself at a fast rate, because I was out surfing again four days later.

The next injury that I experienced happened a couple of weeks into my ministry school in Hawaii. I still was not too interested in pursuing God but was just there to fulfill my heart's desire to surf. On one of my days off from school I was awakened by the sound of waves crashing.

When you hear this sound in Hawaii you know the waves are big. So I jumped up, grabbed my surfboard, and hitched a ride to the nearest great surf spot. When I paddled out, the waves were around twelve feet high, measuring from the front of the wave.

Due to the fast pace of the building of the swells and the fact that Hawaii is an island in the middle of the ocean, the waves can double in height out of the blue. Which is just what happened this particular day. While waiting for a wave, a huge set came rolling in. A set is a group of waves that normally come in three to four waves per set. These sets tend to be shaped better and bigger than other waves. This set was around eighteen to twenty feet. I saw it coming, so I paddled further out to sea in hopes to paddle over the wave before it broke. I barely made it over the first wave, and then the second one came in. I paddled my heart out trying to get over it; the wave was so big, when I looked up at it I could no longer see the sky. Just a wall of water. I almost made it over, but the wave crashed and threw me back over the falls. I slammed into the reef. I tried to work my way up but could not tell which way was up.

Fighting for my life, trying to get a breath of air, I finally found the ground so I pushed off and shot up to the surface just at the right time to get the air I needed before passing out. Right when I got that breath of air, the third wave of the set came crashing down on my head. I instinctively swam down to the bottom and held on to the reef with all my might. The wave went past, and once again I jumped off the bottom of the ocean to get my breath of air I needed. While shooting to the surface, I could not make it any longer without the breath I needed. So I took a breath, but got nothing but water. I finally made it to the surface and spit up all the water that I just had swallowed. I made it up alive but weak, so I found my surfboard and paddled in. Still to this day I would say that that moment was the closest I have ever been to death.

My third injury occurred one week later. I was surfing on my friend's short board. I caught a four-foot wave, but while riding down the wave I went to turn off the top of the wave. My board got caught at the top of the wave and I came falling down. The water where I was surfing was a very shallow spot, so I fell into about six inches of water. All my weight landed on my right toe, which led to me fracturing my foot in two spots. I found myself once again being rushed to the ER with an injury from surfing. God never causes injury or sickness, but He can use what the devil means for evil and turn it around for good. Which is exactly what happened in these cases. After getting treatment, I ended up with a walking boot. The doctor told me, "You cannot walk or surf for two months." This was the worst news that I could have been told. Remember, I was a young man and the reason I even moved to Hawaii to attend a ministry school was to surf. Now the main thing in my life was gone.

The drive back from the ER was a silent one. I began to ponder all that was happening in my life. A pattern of injury was beginning to develop and I needed to know what the cause was. I was just talking with God in my head, telling Him, *I guess I should try out this God thing.* After all, this was what everyone was into here at this school. But I told God, "If I pursue You again, I do not want what I experienced last time. I want a love encounter like You gave my father many years ago. I want my life to be transformed the way his was." I saw the transformation in his life and wanted that for my own. So for the next three days, I would lie in my bed reading books of the Bible and just crying out for this love encounter of a Father who happens to be God.

Finally, my heart was at a place where it could receive this love. I was no longer too strong to find God's love, but that night in my weakness God's love found me. He found me in crisis of weakness. The only way I can explain it is that it felt like I was sitting in my Father's lap and He had both arms wrapped around me, pouring His love into me. "Liquid Love." From that moment, I have not looked back in my journey of love. Never before did I know what the *warring* part of my "warring evangelist" calling meant. But I do know now that the warring part was to be a warrior in love for the souls of the earth. My journey of love led me to the discovery of what Christianity is all about—experiencing the goodness of God's love and making it known to the next person I meet.

My biggest test of this truth came in 2007 when my father died of cancer. He was given three months to live, and he lived thirteen months. Every day in that thirteen-month period, I called him to tell him he was my hero and I commanded cancer to die in the name of Jesus. Then one day a phone call came to get home ASAP if I wanted to see my father alive again. At that time I was attending my second year of Bethel School of Supernatural Ministry at Bethel Church in Redding, California. My encounter with love in Hawaii had so changed me that I had allowed my parents to be a part of the decision of what my life should look like once I graduated YWAM. They went on separate adventures to check out some of the ministry places that could have a deeper effect on what my life purpose was all about. So together we chose Bethel mainly because of the character of one man and his wife.

Bill and Beni Johnson seemed to value people more than ministry. This was a huge factor for my decision, because I had been raised in this environment once my own dad had been changed by his encounter with the Father's love. While in this school I saw hundreds of people healed from all types of sickness and even cancer. It was a normal part of my life to see someone or hear of someone getting healed of cancer.

The whole flight home across America I was crying out in intercession for healing for my father. After what felt like the longest flight of all time, we finally landed. I knew there was something wrong when my mother did not pick my sister, her husband, and me up from the airport. They had their chaplain and lead intercessor, Johnny Lewis, pick us up. My sister needed to stop by Target before heading to the house to see my dad. While they were in the store, Johnny turned around and broke the news to me that my father had passed away while we were traveling across the country.

Before I allowed myself to mourn, I turned my affection toward God, who would become my only source of a Father now. I allowed myself to make a choice to believe that God was sovereign and that no matter what He would find me. I allowed the Father to hold me in His lap and love on me. In the arms of my heavenly Father is where I mourned the death of my earthly one. *If you choose to mourn without the presence of God it will only lead to bitterness.* And I refused to become bitter at a God who was so good that He would love me before I loved Him. A God who would give His Son to a race of people who disdained Him and turned their back against His gift of love. A love that I encountered through my experience growing up in this amazing house of generals. I could never betray this love that so transformed my own life a couple years before.

The last words I heard my father speak were a charge to keeping running the good race. He told me to keep on doing what he was no longer able to do.

The most important lesson I learned growing up in a household of generals was how important it is to understand your own inability to love while being willing to allow the goodness of Father God to find you and change you. This will involve allowing love to find you in your weakness and turn it into your strength. This was the legacy that both of my parents learned the hard way, but it was my dad's willingness to lead his home through his own personal journey of being willing to change the negative learned behaviors that was the catalyst that brought change to our family.

The message I want to leave the world is that I want to be an example of allowing love to change the wounded areas of my life so that I can love God with all my heart and make that love known to the next person I meet. It is a legacy that I am willing to die for. Another main lesson I learned from my parents is that if you want to become a legend you must be willing to have enough courage to embrace the process of change. Watching one life—my dad, who was motivated by the reality that he was loved and that he belonged—changed not only our lives but lives all around the world. The result of this changed life is the restoration of relationships in other families, thus ushering in the next great revival. A revival of Malachi 4:5-6. A revival of restoring the hearts of the parents to their children and the hearts of the children to their parents.

This is life! The only life that I embrace today is receiving love that motivates a person to begin the process of discovery. The discovery that you belong, so you can believe that you are loved and if change is needed in your life you can position yourself for God's love to find you.

My motto in life is, "Belong, Believe, Change."

I know I belong to the Kingdom of Love. I believe that I am unconditionally loved, so I position myself daily for the Father of Love to show me areas of my life that I might need to change so that I can continue to bring this revelation to the world.

You see, I am the next generation of sons who are in our own right on our own path to becoming generals for the next generation. Why? It is the foundation to lasting revival on the earth. *Thy Kingdom come* on earth as it is in heaven!

Thank you, Mom and Dad, for loving me without any conditions and seeing the end result of the great destiny of my life.